HARRIER

Ski-jump to Victory

HARRIER

Ski-jump to Victory

Edited by
John Godden
British Aerospace plc
Kingston-upon-Thames, UK

BRASSEY'S DEFENCE PUBLISHERS
PERGAMON–BRASSEY'S INTERNATIONAL
DEFENSE PUBLISHERS
Members of the Pergamon Group

OXFORD · WASHINGTON D.C. · NEW YORK
TORONTO · SYDNEY · PARIS · FRANKFURT

U.K.	BRASSEY'S PUBLISHERS LTD a member of the Pergamon Group Headington Hill Hall, Oxford OX3 0BW, England
U.S.A.	Pergamon–Brassey's International Defense Publishers, 1340 Old Chain Bridge Road, McLean, Virginia 22101, U.S.A.
	Pergamon Press Inc., Maxwell House, Fairview Park, Elmsford, New York 10523, U.S.A.
CANADA	Pergamon Press Canada Ltd., Suite 104 150 Consumers Road, Willowdale, Ontario M2J 1P9, Canada
AUSTRALIA	Pergamon Press (Aust.) Pty. Ltd., P.O. Box 544, Potts Point, N.S.W. 2011, Australia
FRANCE	Pergamon Press SARL, 24 rue des Ecoles, 75240 Paris, Cedex 05, France
FEDERAL REPUBLIC OF GERMANY	Pergamon Press GmbH, Hammerweg 6, D-6242 Kronberg-Taunus, Federal Republic of Germany

First edition 1983

Library of Congress Cataloging in Publication Data
Main entry under title:
Harrier, ski-jump to victory.
1. Harrier (Jet fighter plane)   I. Godden, John.
UG1242.F5H38 1983 358.4'3 83-21482

British Library Cataloguing in Publication Data
HARRIER ski-jump to victory.
1. Great Britain. Royal Air Force
2. Great Britain. Royal Navy
3. Falkland Islands War, 1982
4. Harrier (Jet fighter plane)
1. Godden, John
997'.11   F3031

ISBN 0-08-031166-0 (Hardcover)
ISBN 0-08-031167-9 (Flexicover)

Cover Illustration
   The cover painting illustrates Commander Nigel Ward's Sea Harrier launching a Sidewinder which gave him his second kill. Original painting by Robert Taylor reproduced with his permission and that of The Military Gallery.

Printed in Great Britain by A. Wheaton & Co. Ltd, Exeter

Foreword

I am particularly glad to have been asked to write the Foreword to this book in which the Harrier's vital contribution to victory in the Falklands campaign is vividly described by those who flew and maintained those astonishingly versatile aircraft. How lucky we were to have the Harrier, because there is no doubt that without it there would have been no possibility of responding to the unprovoked invasion of the islands. Aggression would have been seen to pay, with all that would have meant for the future security of small and unprotected states.

Back in 1966 one of the succession of Defence Reviews to which our Services have been subjected decided that aircraft carriers would be phased out, that the Fleet Air Arm would in future fly only helicopters, and that fixed wing air support for ships at sea would be provided by aircraft flown from shore bases. The naval staff realized the restrictions that this would place on operations and were determined that it should not be. A modified version of the Harrier GR3, already in service with the Royal Air Force, seemed to be the best bet, but there could be no early reversal of so recent a government decision.

The first step was to ensure that there would be suitable ships from which the Harrier could operate. After a long and painful gestation, the "through-deck *cruiser*" was approved and ordered in 1972. Its primary role was to operate the Fleet's big anti-submarine helicopters, but it was designed with a deck from which short take-off aircraft could operate if required.

With the first ship on the building slip and a class of three planned, the Naval Staff turned their attention to making the case for a small flight of modified Harriers for each of these new ships, to provide the Fleet with a quick reaction capability against certain threats which could not be readily dealt with by shore based aircraft. These, in order of priority, were the need to shoot down shadowing aircraft before they could home other attackers on to the Fleet, the need to probe and identify contacts detected by our own shore based reconnaissance aircraft and, lastly, to provide a quick strike capability against enemy surface ships armed with long-range missiles which might evade detection until they were dangerously close.

It took much argument within the Ministry of Defence and with Ministers before the development of the Sea Harrier and the production of a modest number for the Royal Navy was finally approved. Test pilot John Farley flew one of the early prototypes over HMS *Invincible* at her launching by H.M. The Queen in 1977.

Little did anyone imagine, protagonist or antagonist, that the Sea Harrier would prove its value in war so soon. But it was even less imaginable that these aircraft would have to defend a Task

Force carrying out an amphibious landing against attack by shore based fighter bombers, would operate in strikes against shore targets and would provide close support for land forces in the field, none of these tasks on which the case for the provision of the Sea Harrier had been based.

Once again we learnt the old lesson, it is nearly always the unexpected that happens. It pays to be flexible and ready for anything. Those last five words would make a perfect motto for the Harrier.

Admiral of the Fleet Lord Lewin KG, GCB, MVO, DSC, RN

Acknowledgements

The Editor wishes to acknowledge the invaluable assistance of:

The Ministry of Defence
The Royal Navy
The Royal Air Force
British Aerospace
Lt Cdr A. Ogilvy, RN
Cdr T. Gedge, RN
Cdr N. D. Ward, AFC, RN
Cdr A. D. Auld, RN
Lt Cdr R. Bennett, RN
Lt D. Smith, RN
Sqdn Ldr R. D. Iveson, RAF
Sqdn Ldr J. J. Pook, RAF
Flt Sgt R. Cowburn, RAF
Sgt D. Frost, RAF

For photographs:

Ministry of Defence Photographic Unit
Fleet Photographic Unit, HMS *Excellent*
RNAS Yeovilton
Fleet Air Arm Museum, Yeovilton
Lt Cdr R. Bennett, RN
Lt Cdr R. C. Nichol, RN
Flt Lt E. H. Ball, RAF
Lt W. M. Covington, RN
Lt K. White, RN

And the many others, service and civilian, without whose help, suggestions, advice, guidance and willing assistance this book would not have been possible.

The book is dedicated with high regard and respect to those Sea Harrier pilots who did not return from the South Atlantic:
Lt Cdr G. W. J. Batt, DSC, RN
Lt Cdr J. E. Eyton-Jones, RN
Lt W. A. Curtis, RN
Lt N. Taylor, RN

Contents

Acronyms

AAA	Anti-Aircraft Artillery
AIM	Air Interception Missile
AMG-45	Shrike anti-radar missile
AMRAAM	Advanced Medium Range Air-to-Air Missile
ASRAAM	Advanced Short Range Air-to-Air Missile
ASW	Anti-Submarine Warfare
CAP	Combat Air Patrol
CBU	Cluster Bomb Unit
FAA	Fleet Air Arm
FAC	Forward Air Controller
FDO	Flight Deck Officer
FINRAE	Ferranti Inertial Navigation Reference and Attitude Equipment
FRG	Federal Republic of Germany
FOB	Forward Operating Base (San Carlos)
GR1	Designation for first RAF Harrier (Ground attack/Reconnaissance)
GR3	Current RAF Harrier with Laser Ranging and Marked Target Seeker equipment and redesigned nose
INS	Inertial Navigation System
LERX	Leading Edge Root Extensions
LGB	Laser Guided Bomb
MEXE	Military Engineering and Experimental Establishment
MLU	Mid-life Update
NAVHARS	Navigation, Heading and Attitude Reference System
OCU	Operational Conversion Unit
PCB	Plenum Chamber Burning
RCS	Reaction Control System
SCADS	Shipborne Containerised Air Defence System
SNS	Spanish Naval Ship
STOVL	Short Take-off and Vertical Landing
STUFT	Ships Taken Up from Trade (requisitioning of merchant vessels)
USMC	United States Marine Corps
VIFF (thrust)	Vectoring in Forward Flight
VL	Vertical Landing
V/STOL	Vertical/Short Take-off and Landing
VTOL	Vertical Take-off and Landing
WOD	Wind Over Deck

List of Plates

Operation Corporate

Operation Corporate, the code name given to the Falklands campaign, was the first British exercise of military force for many years. To the United Kingdom's armed forces it was also a 'come as you are' war in that it was far removed from the anticipated areas of potential conflict for which the standard peacetime training programmes had catered.

The RN and RAF had, until April 1982, expected their next action to have been NATO-orientated, or perhaps in support of US and local forces in the Middle East. Instead the United Kingdom's services were called upon to repossess a group of sparsely inhabited islands in a military operation that not only was far from home, but had its nearest secure base at Wideawake airfield on Ascension Island, nearly 4,000 miles away, in the middle of the Atlantic and halfway back to the United Kingdom. Tactical air-power in support of any military operation, therefore, could be exercised only by flying from ships or by making use of in-flight re-fuelling. Without integral air cover, deployment of a maritime task force so close to South American mainland bases would have been a suicidal gesture.

The practical answer lay with the RN's Sea Harriers and RAF's Harrier GR3s, a decision that was to prove itself right time and time again during the subsequent weeks. The performance of the Harriers can be summed up by the often quoted statement of Admiral Sir Henry Leach, First Sea Lord and Chief of Naval Staff: ' Without the Sea Harrier there could have been no Task Force. ' As far as the weather conditions and sea states were concerned, it was universally agreed by those who went south that no conventional fixed-wing naval aircraft could have operated in such conditions with adequate safety. On occasions the deck was moving vertically through 30 ft (9 m) and cloud base was often down to 200 ft (60 m), or even 100 ft (30 m) during flying operations. Visibility was typically half a nautical mile or less. No conventional fixed-wing jet fighter operating from ships could possibly have coped with those conditions and survived.

It was the Harrier's ability to close with the ship, using its internal approach aid and Blue Fox radar, at part-jetborne flight speeds of a few tens of knots that provided the primary safety factor and success in bad-weather recovery. This alone totally vindicates the claim that the greatest military contribution made by V/STOL and STOVL aircraft is the VL phase of the operation. In the Harrier, powered lift makes landing safer, easier and more flexible than in any other combat aircraft in service today.

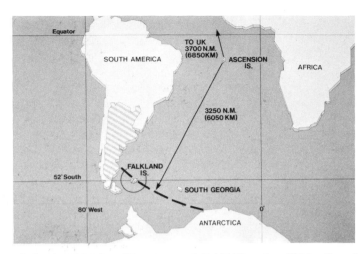

While the RN Sea Harrier and RAF Harrier GR3 pilots had to contend with operating from the cramped conditions of two carriers, the enemy were very close to home – only 400 miles to the west – and were numerically superior. Logistically, therefore, the operation was a considerable problem for the United Kingdom's senior commanders.

The actual events which led to the mobilisation of Task Force 317, politics apart, began just prior to the Argentine invasion of the Falklands and South Georgia. Admiral Sir John Fieldhouse GCB, GBE, subsequently overall Commander of the task force, received orders on March 31 to make covert preparations. Admiral Fieldhouse had just returned from the Mediterranean where RN

Typical sea state encountered by the Task Force during the Falklands campaign.

ships had been taking part in Exercise 'Springtrain'. Before leaving Gibraltar he had ordered Flag Officer First Flotilla, Rear Admiral Sir John ('Sandy') Woodward (at the time the most junior of the RN's three sea-going admirals), to prepare to detach a suitable group of ships, to store ammunition and to be ready to proceed to the South Atlantic. On March 29, the nuclear-powered submarine HMS *Spartan* was detached from Exercise 'Springtrain' and ordered to embark stores and weapons at Gibraltar for deployment to the South Atlantic. The following day a second submarine, HMS *Splendid,* was ordered to deploy from Faslane, and a third, HMS *Conqueror,* sailed a few days later. All were stored within 48 hours. A total of five nuclear-powered submarines, referred to as Task Force 324, were deployed during the campaign, operating under the direct control of Northwood.

Matters came to a head on April 2, 1982 when Argentine forces invaded the Falklands. The invasion force was led by the flagship of the Argentine Navy, the carrier *25 de Mayo.* It was the first and last time the ship played a significant role in the military operations of the campaign. Argentine forces landed, and the small garrison of Royal Marines put up a strong resistance before being ordered to lay down their arms. On April 3, a second Argentine invasion force arrived at Grytviken in South Georgia and again they were met by resistance. This time they lost a Puma helicopter, and the corvette *Guerrico* was severely damaged by an anti-tank weapon. The invasion was immediately condemned by the United Nations Security Council in Resolution 502, which called for the immediate withdrawal of the occupying forces and a peaceful settlement of the dispute.

Only three days after the Argentine invasion of British sovereign territory, the first elements of Task Force 317 had been assembled and had set sail from Portsmouth led by the carrier and flagship, HMS *Hermes,* in company with the new anti-submarine warfare carrier HMS *Invincible,* escort vessels, supply ships and troop ships. It was the largest fleet Britain had sent to sea for many decades and the nostalgic scenes at its departure from the United Kingdom reflected the strength of public support. Thousands crowded into Portsmouth and other ports to make their farewells to the men and ships.

While the main elements of the fleet sailed from the United Kingdom, the selected group of ships from the Mediterranean also weighed anchor and the two units sailed to their rendezvous. Admiral Woodward sailed aboard the county class destroyer HMS *Antrim,* later transferring to HMS *Glamorgan* before finally joining the flagship, HMS *Hermes,* at Ascension Island.

The UK farewells were memorable, but the most remarkable aspect of the sailing of the task force was that though it had been prepared and despatched in only three days it was ready for a campaign that was to last nearly three months. Only with the closest possible co-operation between all three services, the Merchant

HMS Hermes leaving Portsmouth naval base on her way south where she was to become the Task Force's flagship. On her deck can be seen the Sea Harriers of 800 and 899 Squadrons.

Navy, the Royal Dockyards, commercial ports stores and supplies organisations, and the transport elements of both the Ministry of Defence and the Ministry of Trade and Industry could this have been possible. (As an example of the amount of work required, Admiral Woodward's own staff worked six hours on and six hours off for two months. There was to be no 'back-seat driving'.)

Altogether a total of over 111 ships were deployed during the campaign, including 44 warships, 22 Royal Fleet Auxiliaries (RFAs) and 45 merchant ships (the latter with civilian volunteer crews), which alone transported 9,000 personnel, 100,000 tons of freight and 95 aircraft to the South Atlantic. The supply chain carried over 400,000 tons of fuel.

The Argentine Navy strength was listed as consisting of one aircraft carrier, one vintage cruiser, four submarines, two modern Type 42 destroyers (similar to HMS *Coventry* and her sister ship HMS *Sheffield*) and a number of old but well-armed ex US frigates and destroyers. The total made 73 vessels. In addition, the UK task force would have to contend with air attacks from a force listed as having a known strength of at least: 64 A4 Skyhawks, 39 Mirage/ Daggers, 5 Canberras, 60 Pucaras, 8 Puma helicopters, 2 Lynx helicopters, 5 Navy Super Etendards, 2 C130 Hercules and Navy Aermachis.

The anacronym STUFT – ships taken up from trade – was coined during the campaign to designate merchant vessels chartered from the maritime industry and taken into naval service. The ships included tankers, general cargo vessels, offshore support vessels, container ships, deep-sea trawlers and tugs. Some of these ships could be pressed into service immediately, with their standard crew strengths augmented by RN personnel. Others, like the ill-fated *Atlantic Conveyor* required modification or conversion for a new service role, but delays in sending these ships to sea were minimal. Maximum support from the services and industry, utmost priority to task force requirements, the minimum of paper work and no financial restraints were the order of the day. The

4

View of Ascension Island from the Bridge of HMS Hermes. The Task Force gathered here for a few days before continuing the journey south.

liner SS *Canberra,* for example, was earmarked to become a troop-ship. At the time of the invasion she was still at sea in the final stages of a 96-day world cruise. She arrived back in the United Kingdom on the day after the invasion. A scant two days later she was a troopship, fitted with all the necessary equipment and ser-vices as well as two helicopter pads. She sailed 48 hours after arriv-ing back in UK waters. However, *Canberra*'s non-union engine-room crew, which consisted of Pakistani personnel, had to be re-placed and a union crew from Cardiff was substituted. They turned out to be Yemenis!

A vital part of the supply chain was provided by the RAF which moved over 5,800 people and 6,600 tons of stores through Ascension Island in more than 600 sorties by Hercules and VC10 transports. Hercules also made 44 supply drops to the task force – a mission which often called for a round trip of 25 hours.

In early April while the fleet was at sea, diplomatic efforts con-tinued to try to break the political deadlock, but it became more and more apparent that it was impossible to resolve the dispute by peaceful means.

When the various elements of the task force arrived at Ascension Island, Admiral Woodward took the opportunity of transferring men and equipment between ships to ensure maximum utilisation when the time for action came. This 'cross-decking' process continued during the passage from Ascension Island to the Falklands, but much of the preparatory work was done at Ascension. The brief stopover there also allowed some army units to take the opportunity of carrying out manoeuvres with their counterparts from other battalions. In addition Ascension's only airfield, which until now had only seen three aircraft move-ments each week, began to live up to its name – Wideawake. Apart from the daily flights arriving from the United Kingdom, Wide-awake now boasted the permanent residence of 17 RAF Victor tan-kers, three Vulcans, four C130 Hercules, four Nimrods, two to three air defence fighters (initially Harrier GR3s with Side-winders, later Phantoms) and two helicopters. Furthermore, its RAF establishment, previously non-existent, rose to 800. By the end of the campaign over 530 air movements had been made into Ascension, including C130s, VC10s and chartered Belfasts and Boeing 707s.

The net was meanwhile drawing even tighter around the Argentine garrisons on the Falklands and South Georgia. The first move was the announcement of the maritime exclusion zone of 200 miles around the islands against Argentine naval vessels. On April 23, with the task force rapidly approaching the area, the UK Government warned that any approach by Argentine forces which could be seen as a threat would be dealt with appropriately. Two days later came the proof of the United Kingdom's serious intentions when the task force repossessed South Georgia and during the action attacked the Argentine submarine *Santa Fe* on the surface about 5 miles out of Grytviken harbour. Badly damaged, the submarine was later beached. Apart from the psychological blow dealt to the Argentine government, the recapture of South Georgia also provided the fleet with a sheltered anchorage in the vicinity of the forthcoming operations.

On April 29, Argentina was warned that all vessels shadowing the task force were from that moment liable to attack by RN ships or aircraft. The following day brought the imposition of the total exclusion zone – military operations were about to commence.

May 1 saw the first bombing raid by an RAF Vulcan, which attacked Port Stanley airfield at about 0400 hours, dropping a stick of 21 bombs from a height of about 10,000 ft in an oblique run across the runway. As it turned out, only one bomb hit the edge of the runway itself, making a large crater, while the others did extensive damage to the surrounding areas. Only a few hours later came the first Sea Harrier attack with nine aircraft launched at Port Stanley and three on another attack mission to Goose Green. While the carrier-borne combat aircraft were carrying out these

(top) *The crippled Argentine submarine* Santa Fe *alongside the old whaling station jetty. In this photo she is slowly sinking.*

(bottom) *Lt K. White, RN, Engineering Officer of HMS* Antrim, *takes the opportunity of inspecting the forward torpedo room of the* Santa Fe.

opening attacks, the task force, on May 1, carried out a simulated amphibious landing off Port Stanley. This successfully drew the Argentinians and revealed a number of their defensive positions. The same day, the UK Government announced that any Argentine warship or military aircraft detected beyond 12 miles from the mainland would be treated as hostile and liable to attack.

Only one day later, that UK Government announcement was put to the test when HMS *Conqueror,* a nuclear-powered hunter/killer submarine, detected the approach to the total exclusion zone of the Argentine cruiser *General Belgrano* (ex-USS *Phoenix*) together with an escort of two destroyers. Other Argentine naval vessels were also probing the outer limits of the zone and it was clear that this latest force, which was armed with surface-to-surface Exocet missiles and a variety of other modern, sophisticated weaponry, presented a potential threat to the task force. *Belgrano* was therefore attacked and sunk.

On May 4, the task force suffered its first loss – the destroyer HMS *Sheffield* which was on forward radar picket duty about 60 miles to the south-east of the Falklands. She was attacked by two low-flying Super Etendards of the Argentine Navy, which fired two air-to-surface Exocet anti-ship missiles. One of these hit *Sheffield* amidships on the starboard side, causing a number of casualties and destroying the fire main, thus reducing the ship's fire-fighting capability. After four-and-a-half hours, the crew was ordered to abandon ship. Later taken under tow, *Sheffield* sank in heavy seas on May 10.

The day of the air attack on *Sheffield* also brought the second Vulcan attack on the airport and installations surrounding Port Stanley airfield. Three Sea Harriers from 800 Squadron also successfully attacked Pucaras and gun emplacements at Goose Green, but the attacking formation suffered its first casualty when Lt. Nick Taylor RN was shot down by ground fire. It was the first Harrier loss due to enemy action.

Two Sea Harriers of 801 Squadron, operating from *Invincible,* were launched and ordered to intercept a fishing vessel that had been acting suspiciously and was shadowing the fleet. The vessel, the *Narwal,* was first bombed and then successfully straffed by 30 mm gunfire before she surrendered. She was later boarded by a party from the carrier, but subsequently sank.

Meanwhile the naval battle continued, and on May 11, HMS *Alacrity* (a Type 21 frigate), while transiting Falkland Sound at night, spotted a merchant ship off Port Howard. The ship, which was later identified as *Isla de Los Estados,* was illuminated by star shell and challenged. She refused to heave to and *Alacrity* opened fire with her forward mounted 4.5 in gun. *Isla de Los Estados* was hit and blew up. She had been ferrying fuel and supplies to the Argentine garrison.

Sea Harriers played a further role in the naval battle when on May 16 two aircraft located and attacked two transport ships,

7

Bahia Buen Suceso and *Rio Carcarcana*. Both vessels were damaged and immobilised. Later that day the Argentine patrol craft, appropriately named *Islas Malvinas,* and the inter-island ferry *Monsunen* (owned by the Falkland Islands Company) were both attacked, the former being put out of action while the latter, forced to beach, was later refloated and put to use by the British forces.

On May 20, the amphibious forces moved towards Falkland Sound and the San Carlos area – the place chosen for the first landings on East Falkland. While the senior UK commanders were not able to select any point that would render Exocet or air attacks impossible, they could – and did – pick an area that was comparatively easy to defend and would offer a certain amount of shelter for the ships of the task force when the troops and their supporting mountains of equipment were disembarked. The UK commanders knew that the efficiency of the Exocet missile was greatly reduced when its potential targets were close to land or lying in sheltered waters. Although there were other areas that might have been considered to fulfil this requirement, San Carlos was chosen also because it featured deep water – the secondary consideration for the landings. In addition to having deep water and being surrounded by hills, it was diagonally opposite Port Stanley on East Falkland and the nearest Argentine troop dispositions of any great strength were at Darwin or Goose Green, both some 15 miles away.

In the early hours of May 21, the amphibious forces entered Falkland Sound and by the end of that day, over 3,000 troops and 1,000 tons of equipment had been successfully landed in an operation that was virtually unopposed. That afternoon, the first waves of Argentine aircraft appeared. Supersonic Mirage together with fast subsonic A4 Skyhawks came in low over the sea to attack the ships in San Carlos Water and Falkland Sound. There were many Argentine casualties, but they pressed home their attacks in the face of a heavy barrage of missiles, guns and small-arms fire. Three ships were hit, *Antrim, Argonaut* and *Ardent,* the latter repeatedly by bombs, many of which exploded, and these caused her to sink. It was from this point onwards that the Sea Harriers began to prove their real worth in providing air cover over the Falkland Sound area. Their high availability was one of the deciding factors in the establishment of effective combat air patrol (CAP) cover.

Fortunately, on that day the weather conditions were poor and visibility limited. British land forces took their first steps on East Falklands with only minimal resistance and by the following morning, when the skies were clear, 5,000 men had been landed and defensive positions were in the process of being set up.

Sea Harriers on CAP were at this time patrolling the outer perimeter of the layers of defences. Any aggressor aircraft breaking through the Sea Harrier cordon had then to face the second line of defence which was provided by a pair of warships in what was commonly known as the 'missile trap' located off the northern entrance of Falkland Sound. Normally these ships would consist of a Type 42 destroyer armed with Sea Dart and a Type 22 armed with Sea Wolf. Again, any attacking aircraft able to get through the 'missile trap' then had to face another layer of defence – known as the 'gunline', a group of three or four ships inside the entrance to the Sound which would bring to bear every available gun and missile system and throw up a wall of fire at the attacking Argentine aircraft. The 'gunline', however, was not the last line of defence. Within the anchorage itself – nicknamed 'bomb alley' – there were often up to eight store ships or troopships at any one time, and these provided a more than effective final barrage. Sea Cat missiles from the assault ships HMS *Fearless* and HMS *Intrepid* joined with infantry-launched Blowpipe missiles, machine guns and small arms together with the army's Rapier anti-aircraft missile batteries on the hillsides surrounding the shore. The total score of the Rapier surface-to-air missile systems is second only to the Sea Harriers' success and is testimony to its effectiveness.

The Argentine pilots were courageous and pressed home their attacks. On May 21 and May 23 the task force suffered two losses from its 'gunline' when HMS *Ardent* and HMS *Antelope* were hit. Six other ships were hit and damaged between May 21 and May 24. The Argentine attack waves suffered also with the loss of 15 aircraft on May 21, a further 10 on May 23 and another 18 on May 24. These losses are confirmed kills – not probables or possibles. Attrition was not all one-sided, however, as the task force lost another aircraft when a Sea Harrier which had just taken off from *Hermes* blew up, killing the pilot.

In mid-afternoon of May 25 the Argentine Air Force made very determined attacks, pressed home, against units of the task force. That day was Argentina's National Day and increased air activity had been forecast. HMS *Coventry* was the first casualty. A Type 42 destroyer, she had been in the 'missile trap' to the north-west and had successfully controlled Sea Harriers as well as shooting down three aircraft herself. On that day she was attacked by waves of Skyhawks which overwhelmed her defences. Hit by several bombs, which exploded in or near her machinery spaces and vitals, she capsized quickly and the surviving members of her crew were rescued by nearby HMS *Broadsword*.

The air attacks also continued further out at sea, and that day the container ship *Atlantic Conveyor* was to become the second victim. The ship had already delivered an additional eight Sea Harriers and six RAF GR3 Harriers, together with the first Chinook of her helicopter cargo, and was, with the other units of the main body of the task force, en route to San Carlos. Having seen the departure of the Harriers to the two carriers, *Atlantic Conveyor* still carried a vast amount of much needed equipment, including spares, fuel, ammunition, tents to house more than 4,000 men and supplies and other helicopters.

One hour before sunset, the task force received warning of an impending air attack by low-flying Super Etendards. Exocet missiles were launched against the fleet. Diverted by chaff fired from the major warships, the missiles found the large radar image of the defenceless *Atlantic Conveyor*. Two Exocets locked on to the containership and struck her on the starboard side, setting her alight. The flames rapidly spread and she was later abandoned with the loss of 12 lives. Nevertheless, the ship proved to be tough and it was not until some days later that she eventually sank, in heavy seas, while under tow.

A third Exocet attack by Super Etendards was successfully countered on May 30, when the carrier force was closer to the islands supporting the approach of 5th Infantry Brigade troopships. Apart from the successful evasion of the Exocets, which were

A Rapier surface-to-air missile system set up in the Falklands for defence against Argentine air attacks.

(top) *A view from HMS* Hermes *of the task force at sea with HMS* Invincible *surrounded by escorts and followed by replenishment ships.*

The North Sea ferry Norland *is narrowly missed by Argentine bombs in Falkland Sound.*

A Sea Dart missile being fired by a Type 42 destroyer.

HMS Ardent, *part of the 'gunline' inside Falkland Sound, is hit by Argentine bombs. Badly damaged and on fire, she later sank. Alongside her is a Type 12 Rothesay Class frigate.*

11

seen to explode harmlessly, three Skyhawks were shot down on that day, two by Sea Dart missiles and one by a 4.5 in naval gun. British anti-aircraft artillery fire was increasing in strength, now that the army's Rapier surface-to-air-missile systems were beginning to come into action.

The 5th Infantry Brigade, which had sailed from the United Kingdom aboard the luxury Cunard liner *Queen Elizabeth II* transferred from the large ship in Cumberland Bay, South Georgia. The *QE2*, which was kept well clear of any threat area, transferred the troops to the *Canberra* (affectionately known by the troops as the 'Great White Whale') and the motor vessel *Norland,* a North Sea ferry taken up from trade. Assisting in the transshipment were the five converted trawlers of the 11 Mine Countermeasures Squadron. Those same troops disembarked in San Carlos on May 31, and at about the same time preparations were begun to emplace the forward operating base (FOB) at Port San Carlos, which was then assembled and constructed by 11 and 59 Squadrons, Royal Engineers. This consisted of an 850 ft strip of aluminium MEXE (Military Engineering and Experimental Establishment, which had developed this concept in the 1960s) matting, with holding and refuelling loops at one end of the runway.

This site was ready for operations on June 5 and its advantages were immediately felt as Sea Harriers and Harrier GR3s no longer had to fly the many miles back to the task force to refuel. Typically a pair of Sea Harriers would launch from one of the carriers and fly to their designated CAP area over the Falklands. When fuel state ran down, the aircraft flew to San Carlos where they carried out a vertical landing on the temporary strip and were refuelled. This move meant that the two aircraft were again ready and available for CAP at short notice and within a few minutes flying time. Aircraft taking off from the temporary strip would then complete their CAP and subsequently return to their carriers on fuel depletion. The San Carlos strip, however, was used only for refuelling, not

(top*)* *An Argentine Dagger flying low through Falkland Sound. Ahead and above or beyond the fighter-bomber is what appears to be the warhead burst of a surface-to-air missile.*

(bottom*)* *The Forward Operating Base at San Carlos used to refuel Sea Harriers and GR3s, enabling them to operate for extended periods over the Falklands on CAP and ground attack without returning to the ships.*

for ordnance. This temporary strip arrangement is not new, but is also used in the NATO scenario.

Now that the bridgehead was established, the advance to Port Stanley became the next major objective and RAF Harriers carried out ground attacks in support of army attacks, typically the paratroopers' attacks on Goose Green where Harriers were used to 'soften up' the defenders. In addition, the RAF's Vulcan force added their weight to this 'softening-up' process with raids on May 31 and June 3 against radar installations in the vicinity of Port Stanley, using AMG-45 Shrike radar-homing missiles, with some success.

In addition, on June 1 and again a week later, two pairs of RAF Harrier GR3s were ferried from Ascension Island direct to the fleet to reinforce the RAF's ground-attack force. These aircraft had flown two nine-hour sectors from the United Kingdom with only an overnight stop at Ascension, refuelling in flight from RAF Victor tankers. After their last 'plug-in' well to the north of the task force, the pairs of Harriers flew on alone and unshepherded until they were met by Sea Harriers launched from the carriers. The formations then made their own way to the ships, where the RAF pilots in the GR3s, at the end of their nine-hour mission, made their first ever deck landings on Hermes.

On June 8, tragedy struck the task force when the Royal Fleet Auxiliaries, *Sir Galahad* and *Sir Tristram,* were hit by Argentine aircraft at Fitzroy. Both ships were abandoned, with the loss of 50 lives. Later that day the balance was somewhat restored when two patrolling Sea Harriers shot down four Mirages over Choiseul Sound.

The main battle for Port Stanley began on June 11–12, and during this period the RAF launched the first raids with Harriers carrying two Paveway laser guided bombs (LGBs). These attacks

The gutted wreck of Atlantic Conveyor *after the Exocet attack in which 12 men died including her Master, Captain North. Still aboard the ship were vital stores required by the Task Force, including a spare Pegasus engine and tent accommodation destined for the troops on land.*

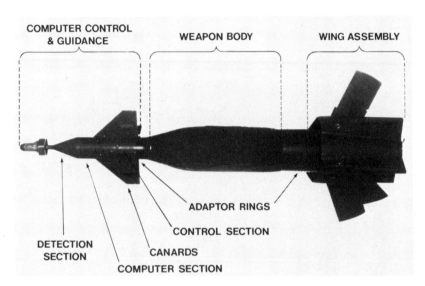

COMPUTER CONTROL & GUIDANCE • WEAPON BODY • WING ASSEMBLY

ADAPTOR RINGS
CONTROL SECTION
DETECTION SECTION
CANARDS
COMPUTER SECTION

(top) *The charred remains of the LSL* Sir Tristram.

(right) *Laser Guided Bomb.*

(bottom) *A Ferranti Laser Designator, as used by the army to enable pin-point accuracy using "smart bombs".*

were carried out with the close co-operation of forward air controllers, and the GR3s, carrying a pair of 1,000 lb bombs fitted with the Paveway laser seeking and guidance kit, were briefed to attack using a loft bombing mode. Initially these attacks met with limited success due to the unfamiliarity of the pilots and the forward air controllers with the equipment. Once this problem had been overcome, however, the 1,000 lb Paveway LGBs, produced by Portsmouth Aviation using equipment from the United States, proved themselves to be highly accurate and very effective.

The method of operation requires a controller to 'illuminate' the target using a Ferranti laser designator – of which eight were sent to the South Atlantic. The bomb, released by the Harrier in a loft release launch some 6–7 km distant from the target, rises through its trajectory to its peak at about 1,500 ft and then begins to fall in the general direction of the target. At this critical point of the attack, the controller should illuminate the target and the bomb will then 'lock on' to the laser light reflected from the target and attempt to home in on the signal source. The controller's role is particularly important as the target must be illuminated only after a set number of seconds from bomb release. This latter depends on the speed of the attacking aircraft, the distance from re-

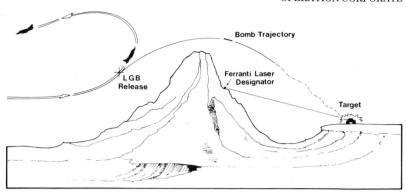

Bomb Trajectory

LGB
Release

Ferranti Laser
Designator

Target

*This diagram shows a typical
loft bombing technique using
a Laser Guided Bomb.*

lease to impact, and so on. Should the target be illuminated while
the bomb is on its upward trajectory, the Paveway sensors will pick
up the reflections and attempt to guide the bomb to the source too
early. In effect this causes the bomb to depart early from its ballistic trajectory and commence an early descent, falling short of its
target. Once its ballistic trajectory has been lost the LGB cannot
regain its original flight path as its movable control fins are only
capable of altering its course by a few degrees; it is not a very good
glider.

The first attack in which a Paveway LGB was used was the day
before the Argentine surrender during the fighting around
Tumbledown Mountain. Lasers were mounted by forward air controllers on nearby Two Sisters Mountain, and Argentine infantry
positions and guns were picked as the target. The attacking RAF
GR3s, with two 1,000 lb LGBs on the outer underwing pylons made
their approach to Tumbledown from the south-east and were
shielded from the Argentine positions by Mount Harriet. The attack on Tumbledown was to be made from behind Mount Harriet
and the pilot would not even see his target until after weapon release. Approaching at approximately 550 knots and 500 ft, the
Harrier pulled up into a shallow zoom behind the mountain, releasing the bomb at an elevation of about 30 degrees. The weapon
continued on its ballistic trajectory up and over the peak and on towards the target. Unfortunately this attack failed as the controller
illuminated the target too soon and the bomb fell well short of it. A
second run was made with the second bomb and this time the controller illuminated the target at the correct time, when the bomb
was at its maximum height. The 1,000 lb bomb made a direct hit on
the target.

A second attack was mounted on Argentine infantry positions
later that day. Again the first bomb fell short for the same reason
as in the earlier attack, but as with the second run on the previous
attack, the second release was a direct hit also, this time on an
Argentine howitzer.

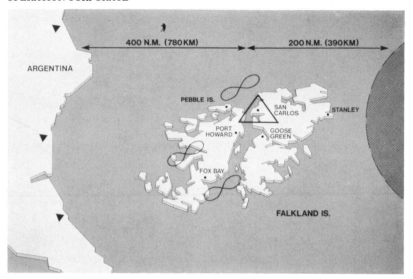

Combat Air Patrol Areas (CAP).

Following this satisfactory display of air/ground co-ordination, further attacks were planned for the following day. RAF Harriers armed with Paveway LGBs launched from HMS *Hermes* for an attack on the Argentine Headquarters on Sapper Hill. It was while the aircraft were flying towards the island that General Menendez, the Argentine commander in the Falklands, agreed to surrender. The Harrier attack was called off, and a message was received by the attacking aircraft when it was only ten minutes away from bomb release.

It is understood that prior to these attacks, Harriers had attempted a high-level bombing mission against Port Stanley airfield using the LGBs. High level was chosen to keep the aircraft out of range of the Argentine gun and surface-to-air- missile defences. While the first Harrier released a single bomb, a second aircraft attempted to illuminate the runway with its own nose-mounted Ferranti laser ranger and marked target seeker. On paper the systems seem to be compatible, but in practical terms they are not, as this attack proved. The bomb failed to achieve a positive target lock. But while the runway attack failed, the sorties co-ordinated by forward air controllers proved the validity of the LGB method of attack, and interest in LGBs using the loft delivery mode has increased as far as RAF operations in NATO central Europe are concerned. In the Falklands campaign, there was no further occasion when this method could be used, for on June 13–14 hostilities ceased.

FALKLANDS - Harrier Force Deployed

TRANSIT METHOD	RN Sea Harriers	RAF Harrier GR3s
EMBARKED IN UK: HMS Hermes HMS Invincible	12 8	— —
FLOWN* UK TO ASCENSION IS. then ★ via Atlantic Conveyor to 52°S. (Flown off to VL on carriers.) ★ via Contender Bezant to 52°S. (Flown off to Pt. Stanley)	8 —	6 4
FLOWN* UK TO LAT. 52°S. with intermediate landing at Ascension Is. VL on H.M.S Hermes	—	4
TOTALS	28	14

* Refuelled in flight using
RAF Victor tankers

UK – Ascension Is. ≏ 3700 n.m. (6850 km)
Ascension Is. – Falkland Is. ≏ 3250 n.m. (6050 km)

FALKLANDS - Harrier Force Missions

Sea Harrier

Intercept — CAP & deck alert
Recce — Sea and land
Strike — Loft bombing
Medium level bombing
Ground attack
Radar suppression

Harrier GR 3

Recce — with photo pod
Strike

Ground attack
Radar suppression

OPERATIONAL FLYING
★ 2000+ sorties south of Ascension Is.
Some 1650 sorties within TEZ
★ Combat missions:
• Sea – 1100+ CAP sorties
Harrier – 90 offensive support
– 125 ground attack and
tactical reconnaissance
★ Flying rate:
• approx 55 hrs/a/c/month
• up to 6 sorties / a/c / day
• 3-4 sorties/pilot/day
• up to 10 hrs/day in cockpit
★ Pilot-to-aircraft ratio: 1·2 initially
1·4 later
★ Aircraft availability at beginning
of each day: 95%
★ Only 1% of planned missions not
achieved through unserviceability

FALKLANDS - Harrier Force Losses

LOSSES DUE TO	RN Sea Harriers		RAF Harrier GR3s	
	Aircraft lost	Pilots killed	Aircraft lost	Pilots killed
HOSTILE ACTION Ground defences	2	1	3	—
Air-to-Air combat	NONE		NONE	
OTHER CAUSES Slid off deck	1	—	—	—
Hit sea after launch	1	1	—	—
Collided or flew into sea	2	2	—	—
TOTALS	6	4	3	—

There were 1650 operational sorties within the TEZ.
Overall loss rate/sortie 0·61%
Operational loss rate/sortie 0·8%
Known ejection attempts success rate 100%

FALKLANDS - Argentine Air Losses (1)

Argentine Order of Battle	
Air Force	220
Navy	20

Weapon Type	Confirmed	Probable
Sea Harrier	20	3
SAM	45	10
Other	7	1
Destroyed on ground or captured	31	
TOTAL	**103**	**14**

Note :

A probable kill is one where there are reasonable grounds to believe an aircraft was destroyed, but there is insufficient weight of collateral evidence to claim a confirmed kill.

Argentine Air Losses

OFFICIAL UK GOVERNMENT FIGURES REPRODUCED FROM THE WHITE PAPER, DECEMBER 1982 CMND 8758 THE FALKLANDS CAMPAIGN: THE LESSONS

Sea Harrier Kills	Confirmed	Probable
Mirage	12	1
A4 Skyhawk	5	
Canberra	1	
Pucara	1	
Helicopter	1	2
TOTAL	**20**	**3**

	Confirmed	Probable
Total missile kills	45	10
Total gunfire kills	7	1
Destroyed on ground or captured	31	
TOTAL	**83**	**11**

	Confirmed	**Probable**
GRAND TOTAL	**103**	**14**

As a result of information being made public since the Government White Paper, Royal Navy Sea Harriers have been unofficially credited with at least 23 kills, including a C130 Hercules.

Plate 1

The eight Sea Harriers of 809 Naval Air Squadron lined up at RNAS Yeovilton in 1982 prior to departure for Ascension and the South Atlantic.

An RAF Harrier GR3 in a hide in Germany. Concealed from the air, this aircraft can be airborne in minutes to provide rapid support to ground forces.

Plate 2

Three RAF GR3s over Sardinia during a live weapon training detachment in 1976.

Sea Harriers in post-Falklands colours: one from each Naval Air Squadron. From the top: 899, 801 and 800.

Squadron Leader Bob Iveson RAF

for which he was mentioned in despatches.

Squadron Leader Bob Iveson (35), Flight Commander in No. 1 (F) Squadron, RAF Wittering, Northants, is married and has a son and daughter. Along with other pilots of No. 1 (F) Squadron, he was deployed to the Falklands to operate with their Harrier GR3s primarily in ground attack fire support for land-based military operations in the campaign.

By the Easter weekend, 1982, it became apparent that our services would be required. On Tuesday, April 13, I should have been in Canada with eight aircraft of No. 1 (F) Squadron, taking part in a major exercise there entitled Maple Flag 9, but I was taken out of the loop of pilots destined to go there.

Early preparations for RAF deployment to the Falklands went ahead without me. I, instead, was sent to Liverpool to inspect the then laid-up Cunard containership, *Atlantic Conveyor,* and together with other officers decided that the ship could, in fact, carry helicopters and Harriers to the South Atlantic, operating the former, but not the Harriers, during the course of the voyage.

The group discussed many options as well as time-scales involved in the proposed conversion of this ship. Even the largest containership has cabin space for only some 30 crew – this is clearly insufficient when one takes into account the number of pilots and aircraft support crews needed, as well as the ship's crew itself which would not necessarily alter in number from the original ship's complement.

In view of the numbers of GR3 Harriers involved – a total of six were to be landed on *Atlantic Conveyor* at a later date, together with eight Sea Harriers of 809 RN Squadron and a number of helicopters – it became apparent that the logistics problem would prevent us from operating the Harriers regularly while the ship was under way. There would not even be a chance for some of the pilots to practise landing on a ship while at sea. *Atlantic Conveyor* would simply have to be used as a Harrier ferry vessel with the aircraft being ferried as deck cargo.

The ship steamed from Liverpool, her home port, to Devonport where the Royal Navy dockyard got to work, converting her for this new role. In addition to carrying our RAF Harriers and RN Sea Harriers, with a variety of helicopters, *Atlantic Conveyor* was also to carry a vast amount of military stores, both for land-based and sea-based operations. Within the ship's hull there was also stowed a complete packaged tented town to be used to house approximately 4,000 troops. *Atlantic Conveyor* also carried our RAF BL–755 cluster bomb units (CBUs), bombs and other required weaponry, for use by both our own Harriers and the RN Sea Harriers.

Conversion completed, the ship left Devonport and sailed without any Harriers for Ascension Island, though she was carrying a number of key RAF personnel on board. The Harriers of No. 1 (F) Squadron left for Ascension Island independently, flying first from our base at RAF Wittering to St Mawgan in Cornwall and from there to Ascension Island with a flying time of about nine-and-a-half hours, refuelling in flight from RAF Victor tankers.

The ferry flights were spread over three days, May 3, 4 and 5, with three Harriers departing on each day. During my ferry flight, we undertook five refuellings en route on this 3,500 nm (6,000 km) leg. We could have got away with only three 'top-ups', but as an extra safety factor we operated so as never to deplete our fuel level below that required for a diversion to a friendly shore base if the next 'top-up' failed to provide additional fuel due to system malfunction. Victor tankers were used and the refuellings took place at 30,000–32,000 ft at speeds of Mach .8. The Harrier GR3s were carrying 330 gallon ferry tanks on the in-board pylons and empty 100 gallons tanks on the out-board pylons. These latter would be used during our combat sorties since the task force was positioned a considerable distance east of the Falkland Islands. The 330 gallon tanks would be discarded after arrival as they were not required once the ferry flight was complete.

A deck view in Atlantic Conveyor *shows RN Sea Harriers parked between the rows of containers.*

A GR3 refuels from a Victor tanker.

At Ascension Island, a day after all the Harriers had arrived, six GR3s air taxied from Wideawake airfield over to *Atlantic Conveyor* and landed vertically on board, using the specially-built VTOL landing pad situated on her deck towards the bows, just aft of the forward mast. This VTOL spot allowed the aircraft to land, turn aft and taxi through a gap in the container walls towards the bridge superstructure, where they were marshalled and parked. Three Harriers of No. 1 Squadron were left on Ascension Island, as there was a threat – albeit a slight one – of a possible air attack. In addition to the six Harriers of No. 1 Squadron, *Atlantic Conveyor* also took aboard eight Sea Harriers of 809 Squadron, plus Chinook and Wessex helicopters. All these made for a very crowded ship.

As for RAF and RN crews there was a total of 8 pilots and 18 ground crew for the RAF Harriers alone. However, to ease the accommodation problems, some of the personnel were embarked in the North Sea ferry *Norland.*

It was the first time most of the pilots had ever landed their Harriers on board a ship at sea. Many had not even seen a carrier from their cockpit in flight. But calm sea conditions with little wind and a steady ship at anchor offshore provided an ideal vertical landing pad and no difficulties were experienced in these first-ever deck landings.

The Chinooks were from 18 Squadron RAF and had been landed-on at Devonport. On May 18, *Atlantic Conveyor* closed the task force in latitude 52 South, and when within sight the Harriers and Sea Harriers were ferried by a short VTOL flight to their respective carriers. Most, including all the GR3s went to *Hermes.*

This cross-deck operation was carried out in good weather, so some of our pilots still had to experience a vertical landing onto a 'live' flight deck – an experience which was inevitably going to arise from the bad weather generally prevailing in the South Atlantic.

Wing Commander Peter Squire led the GR3s from *Atlantic Conveyor* on to their new home, but two aircraft of No. 1 Squadron were unserviceable due to very minor defects (everything had to be perfect). These two did not leave *Atlantic Conveyor* for *Hermes* until the next day, May 19. Unlike the earlier Harrier ferry hops to *Hermes,* these last two GR3s had to fly firstly to HMS *Invincible,* as the flagship was by then out of range. Having landed on board *Invincible,* the two GR3s were refuelled, turned round rapidly and then flew on to their new base ship, *Hermes,* which was by then much closer to the Falklands.

On May 19, a number of carrier-based practice sorties were held to acclimatise the RAF pilots to their new roles – operating from a carrier at sea and under war conditions. Typically this involved two against one in air-to-air combat, though our role was destined to be ground attack, releasing the RN's Sea Harriers for combat air patrols (CAP). But on May 20, No. 1 (F) Squadron went to war for the first time, after the smallest amount of training for this particular role. The first mission, led by the Commanding Officer, Wing Commander Peter Squire, with me as his number two and Squadron Leader Jerry Pook (both of us flight commanders) also in the formation, was briefed for an attack on military installations in the Fox Bay area. These consisted of fuel and oil reserves for the Argentinian forces.

All the Harriers involved carried BL–755 cluster bomb units (CBUs) and we made one fast low pass over the target, releasing the ordnance. We observed secondary explosions – caused by the CBUs going off – and this was followed by the eruption of a massive fireball: the dump had exploded.

Operationally it was fairly straightforward but it was, after all, the first wartime action by No. 1 Squadron since World War II and we considered it to be a great success. As in any part of the South Atlantic at that time of year, the weather was in general bad and the visibility variable. At times we had a cloud base that was down to 100 ft, but one could fly a short way out of that area to find the cloud base to be non-existent (i.e. down to the sea). One could also fly at 25,000 ft with maximum visibility over the same area!

On our return from this first attack we went through cloud off the North Coast of East Falkland, where the weather was a bit better than West Falkland, and managed to locate the task force and our base ship, to make a carrier-controlled landing.

We had made our attack at high speed and low level and we did not see any anti-aircraft artillery. But, while this first ground attack mission was considered a great success, with a fuel dump hit in the first run, day two (May 21) proved that the wheel of fate had turned. No. 1 Squadron suffered its first casualty. Flight Lieutenant Geoff Glover was shot down over Port Howard when carrying out an attack on Argentinian positions. Whilst carrying out his attack, Geoff was hit by ground fire. On *Hermes* morale took a knock, even though we had expected something like this. We did not know at that time whether Geoff had in fact survived, and this obviously affected us deeply.

The following day, No. 1 Squadron flew to Goose Green where four Harriers attacked the defences consisting of slit trenches, fox

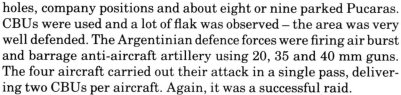

(top) *Wg Cdr Peter Squire, CO of No. 1 (F) Squadron, lands the first GR3 aboard HMS* Hermes.

(bottom) *A mix of Sea Harriers and GR3s on the deck of HMS* Hermes.

holes, company positions and about eight or nine parked Pucaras. CBUs were used and a lot of flak was observed – the area was very well defended. The Argentinian defence forces were firing air burst and barrage anti-aircraft artillery using 20, 35 and 40 mm guns. The four aircraft carried out their attack in a single pass, delivering two CBUs per aircraft. Again, it was a successful raid.

On May 24, No. 1 Squadron attacked Port Stanley airfield itself – the hub of the Argentinian defence forces and the area where one could expect the maximum defence capability. On this occasion a total of six aircraft were used – four GR3s and two Sea Harriers. I led the attack. The Sea Harriers used 1,000 lb bombs fused for air burst to keep down the heads of the defenders. The two Sea Harriers attacked from the sea, while we completed a circuit to approach the same target from the opposite direction – over the land. We hugged the contours as close as possible – that is what we are trained to do – and our GR3 formation was not detected by the defences until it was too late for them to react.

We dropped 1,000 lb retarded bombs and we hit the runway several times, as well as knocking out a couple of Pucaras and a helicopter into the bargain. There was a fair amount of flak but, surprisingly, not as heavy as the fire power we had experienced at Goose Green. We caught the defenders totally by surprise, coming in as we did from the other direction to the attack delivered by the Sea Harriers. All the anti-aircraft guns were pointing out to sea, not in our direction. In general terms, the anti-aircraft artillery aiming was not terribly accurate and fire was fairly spasmodic, although we all admitted, following that attack, that the barrage fire and small arms weapons were heavy and efficient. It turned out afterwards that quite a few ground-to-air-missiles had been fired at us, including Roland, but none of them hit.

Following the attack, we made our escape at high speed and at very low level, skimming only a few feet above the sea on our way out. I am told that missiles did in fact follow us, but observers have told me that some dived into the sea and some shot straight up, as we disappeared from the missile's 'lock' when we followed the ground's contours. It was an interesting sortie.

The following day was a bad one for the task force; as *Atlantic Conveyor* was hit by an air-launched Exocet. It was a great blow to us because we had all got to know Captain Ian North (called Captain Birdseye by the Press, but very fondly known as Father Christmas by those on board his ship) and his very professional Merchant Navy crew. He was a very nice man and we mourned his loss. From *Hermes* we could see his ship dying in the distance. Some of her crew were brought over to us and of all the equipment on board, apart from the Harriers flown off earlier, only one Chinook managed to get away. We had an enormous amount of respect for *Atlantic Conveyor*'s crew, so much that it is hard to describe how we felt.

On May 26 we were still at the peak of the Argentinian Air Force attacks on our landing forces. With the loss of *Atlantic Conveyor* we knew we had lost a large number of CBUs, 1,000 lb bombs, Chinooks and support equipment on her deck and in her holds, all of this equipment vital to our forthcoming military push on land. But our ground attack missions in support of the army went on as usual, and on May 26 we managed to avenge Geoff Glover. We returned to Port Howard, attacking the same ground where he had been shot down. It was an extremely good attack. We used CBUs along two lines of Argentinian positions and we could see the bombs exploding right along the lines with 100 per cent accuracy.

During the run-in to that target the cloud base was less than 100 ft, and it was a very interesting approach at that height. The attack was well planned and no anti-aircraft artillery was observed. We did have an uninvolved observer at the time. A Sea Harrier on CAP at about 25,000 ft followed us over the target to watch the results. He told us by radio that we were on track for the target. We approached at high speed at very low level, following the contours of the ground as we had been trained to do in the European theatre. As we topped the hill just prior to the target there it was, right in front of us, dead in line with our approach.

The following day, May 27, the 2nd Parachute Regiment began their advance on Darwin and Goose Green. We were told that we might be needed to provide ground attack fire support for their advance, and it would be in high risk areas (i.e. well-defended).

I was sitting in my cockpit on the deck of *Hermes* at five minutes cockpit alert. The scramble alarm went and within a very short time the Harrier was roaring along the flight deck to launch up the ski-jump. We formed up and flew at high level towards our briefed targets. Information from the land forces was, at that time, rather sparse and we were not in contact with the forward air controller (FAC). So we had no close control by radio near the target. We did have bare details of the target types and approximate positions, however.

My priority target was infantry defence positions and they proved particularly hard to see. On my first pass I was virtually over the target and away before I spotted the positions. My own specific target was a single Argentine field gun – not the easiest of targets at the best of times, but I was almost on top when I spotted it.

I called up my number two who was slightly behind me, and had sufficient time to line up for an attack – he got the CBUs away on his first pass and I think was on target. Being a priority target, I turned and ran in a second time, but again I spotted it too late – an isolated gun is a pretty difficult target to acquire visually, especially at low level. So rather than continue to make fruitless passes over the primary target, I decided to divert to the secondary target – still of importance. I did not want my number two to accompany me to that second target – after all I was still 'bombed up' and he was not, so why give the Argentinians two aircraft to shoot at? No point, so I carried on alone.

For my third pass over enemy positions, my target was a company-defended position consisting of slit trenches and foxholes. I attacked and experienced very heavy flak throughout. Without assistance from a FAC or target marker, the attack was even more difficult. I dropped the bombs and the formation reformed to return to the flagship – to another rather gamey landing.

But after landing, the day's activities were clearly not yet over as we were ordered to re-arm and turn round quickly for a second go at the same targets. That reinforced my own opinion that the Paratroopers were in fact in trouble.

Turnround time was kept to a minimum even allowing for the fact that *Hermes* was operating 21 Harriers and each one on the flight deck was being turned round as fast as possible – Sea Harriers for CAP and ours for ground attack. We all had to take our place in the replenishment and re-arming queue.

Three Argentine soldiers are startled by the low-flying GR3 from which this photograph came. The soldier on the right is carrying what appears to be a Blowpipe SAM launcher.

Back again into our cockpits and we waited for our launch time. Launch up the ski-jump and back over the Falklands once more.

Again there was no FAC assistance and several targets were in the offing. I was told to go for a different gun, but I neither saw it nor received any detailed information about its precise location. It was a secondary target anyway. But I went round for a second look and on that pass I detected company positions. I released my CBUs and it was, I think, a good attack. But, because I assumed the Paratroopers were in trouble and needed every form of assistance they could get, I decided that I would give this attack everything I had. So I came in again, low and fast to use by 30 mm guns. Normally this is tactically inadvisable, but in view of the ground situation I felt it was a must.

The gun attack worked well, giving the Argentine troops a long burst right along their trenches before pulling off. I had reversed my flight path down to 100 ft when I felt hits, one closely followed by the other. They must have been fairly heavy calibre as the shock through the aircraft was very noticeable – two heavy thumps. Almost immediately the fire warning light came on, and I detected fumes in the cockpit. Suddenly the controls froze completely – I thought I must have been hit in both the hydraulic control systems. But shortly after they cleared again, but when I carried out a rapid visual cockpit check I found I was losing hydraulic pressure at an alarming rate.

I punched the fire extinguisher system and checked in the mirror, looking along the top of the aircraft where I saw flames. Smoke then started pouring into the cockpit. Then the controls went slack and the aircraft went into a dive. I managed to arrest the angle by vectoring the engine nozzles (this provides a very powerful nose-up trim change which can be used to great effect in air combat) and the aircraft nose picked up. Although I had by then corrected the angle of dive, flames now started licking into the cockpit itself.

The Pegasus engine was still running in fine style, but it was obviously a situation that I could not sustain without any usable flying control, so I pulled the ejection handle. I must have passed out for a few seconds because the next thing I knew I was flying horizontally through the air and going straight for a fireball – my burning aircraft.

There were a few tense moments at that point, but fortunately the main chute opened and I was dropping clear of the fireball. I think I was on the chute only for about five or ten seconds – it was very quick indeed. As I landed I could not see very well, as my eyes were affected by the high speed wind blasting at my face during the ejection. I did know, however, that I was on the wrong side of the lines – behind the Argentinian frontline forces. I saw dots coming down the hill in the distance and my immediate reaction was that they were enemy troops looking for me.

On reflection later I thought they could have been animals, but one cannot be too careful in a situation like that. At that range, with my eyes streaming, I could not make out what they were so I did the obvious thing, I cleared off in the other direction, and much later that evening I found a deserted farmhouse.

I knew the Argentinians were looking for me as a Huey helicopter with a big searchlight came towards me that evening. He began hovering over one spot, so I think he must have found the aircraft's remains. Even though it was pitch black, I recognised that it was a Huey by the rather distinctive sound made by its rotor blades which I knew from my tour flying AV–8A Harriers in the US Marine Corps.

He moved away from the spot where he had been hovering and came towards me. Fortunately, at that moment, the night attack on Goose Green started up and he moved off, not wanting to be caught in the open with all that ordnance flying around.

I spent the following two days either in the heather or in the farmhouse at night, as it was bitterly cold and any form of shelter was welcome. I was eventually picked up on May 29 by a Royal Marine, flying an army Gazelle helicopter. He had been searching for me and took me back to 3rd Brigade Headquarters where I was made royally welcome by the officers and men. Next day I was ferried back to *Hermes* by a Royal Navy Sea King helicopter. Needless to say, the 'welcome home' back on board was also very congenial.

Due to minor injuries received during ejection, I was laid off flying for a few days, and next took to the air on June 5 on a sortie to Port San Carlos, where we had by then established an 850 ft metal runway with refuelling facilities. From there we flew close air support missions on Port Stanley, but no targets were called for us. Two other pilots flew the aircraft back from Port San Carlos to the ship and I stayed with a family locally for two days. It was great to have a real bed that did not heave up and down. The family were marvellous and I enjoyed my stay – it was either that or two days in trenches, not much of a choice.

I flew out from the metal strip on June 7 and it was very uneventful except that by this time my back was beginning to give me trouble and I was 'grounded' by the *Hermes'* medics and on June 11 sent back to the United Kingdom. The first part of the journey, to Ascension Island, was made on the BP tanker, *British Trent* and also on board were some survivors of the Royal Fleet Auxiliary *Sir Tristram* which had been bombed in the Bluff Cove landings. I finally touched home soil on June 24, the last part of the journey being made by VC–10. I was the first pilot of No. 1 Squadron to return home to Wittering.

Personally speaking I think there were several significant factors that came out of the operations in the Falklands, particularly in relation to the Harrier. First and most important there was no other aircraft in the world capable of carrying out this type of operation, given that we had no large aircraft carriers or friendly bases nearby. Without these aircraft we could not have carried out this operation in the way we did.

A Royal Navy Sea King helicopter takes off from HMS Hermes.

Our own defence policies had not really taken an operation of this nature into account. We in the RAF are geared to fighting an action from land bases in NATO, not a conflict 8,000 miles from home, operating from carriers. But even though the RAF Harrier force is land-based, and non-naval trained pilots, the actual flying and the launch and recovery from (to us) strange ships at sea proved no problem at all.

It says a great deal for the flexibility of the Harrier that in only half a day we trained pilots, some of whom had never before seen a carrier, to land on vertically and launch using a ski-jump (also for the first time). Without the performance boost given by the ski-jump launch we would not have been able to carry the fuel and ordnance to do our job.

It should not be forgotten that while the aircraft itself was the lynchpin of our air operations, our pilot training has been proved in a combat situation to be second to none. All the RAF pilots were completely prepared for this sort of actual combat scenario. It is only by training the RAF pilots in peacetime to such a high standard of readiness that we could have operated under these conditions at latitude 52 South. There was no delay in changing our role from land to sea, and the weapons system still had a 100 per cent effectiveness.

All of us were agreeably pleased with the high level of serviceability of the Harriers, with minimum maintenance required to the aircraft. We only had a ground crew (or should I say deck crew) of 18 men who handled 6 aircraft. But at all times we had 4 to 5 aircraft ready for action, despite the repairs required overnight by the Harriers' exposure in our attack roles to a great deal of small arms fire and a few larger-calibre shells as well.

Battle damage repair schedules and procedures worked very well. In total the GR3s collected about 30 to 40 hits, with some aircraft returning with 5 or 6 holes. One came back with its tail overheating where a bullet had gone through its rear reaction control ducting, and the aircraft appeared to be on the point of catching fire by the time it landed vertically on *Hermes'* deck. We also discovered that the Harriers windshield can withstand bullet impact.

The FINRAE unit used aboard HMS Hermes *to align the GR3's inertial navigation and attitude reference platform.*

Back in the UK, At RAF Wittering, GR3s were being modified to carry Sidewinder missiles for air defence.

We used Ferranti inertial navigation reference and attitude equipment (FINRAE) on board to align our inertial platforms, but primarily we employed visual navigation as the INAS could not be aligned to full land-based accuracy for which the aircraft needs to be absolutely still. We also used the head-up-display reversionary weapon aiming sight, which worked well.

In total we carried out 130 attack sorties and lost three aircraft, all to ground fire. A fourth Harrier crashed during vertical landing at the 850 ft metal runway at San Carlos. This mishap stemmed from damage by small arms fire. Fortunately as we now know, none of the RAF pilots was lost. The only one missing was Geoff Glover and we knew he was a prisoner of war in Argentina.

At the outset, we ensured that our pilots were a close-knit team. Many had recently left the squadron to go to other postings, and were brought back from their new duties – consequently we didn't have to work up as a team, or get to know each other and identify one another's particular expertise or thinking. That was a great advantage. We operated in the air making full use of that personal knowledge. Although the GR3s are now fitted with Sidewinder, the RN preferred that their Sea Harriers would carry out the defensive fighter role and therefore we would not be needed for these duties.

Our speciality was ground attack in which all of us were highly trained: even so we would have liked to take over one or two CAPs just to see what they're like and perhaps gain experience in air combat. As it was, following the end of hostilities after our deployment ashore to Port Stanley, Harrier GR3s of No. 1 Squadron took over the role of air defence of the area, to assist the RN's Sea Harriers. The RAF Harrier force has yet to be proven in air combat, but we have no reason to believe the Harrier GR3 will not be as successful as the Sea Harrier.

Commander
Nigel Ward DSC, AFC, RN

Commander Nigel ('Sharkey') Ward was Commanding Officer of 801 Naval Air Squadron, operating from HMS *Invincible*.

The Battle for the Falklands, 1982, has received so much varied publicity in the past few months that it is now sometimes difficult to discern the wood from the trees. The proliferation of articles in the press and the coverage in the media in general has tended to disguise certain facts and to rely to some degree on conjecture. However, my own memories of the confrontation remain, for the most part, vivid and are ones which continue to give me great pride in my squadron, my ship and the Royal Navy as a whole. It would probably require a book to relate all my detailed thoughts on the campaign and so, in this account, I shall confine myself to just a few comments of my own and my squadron's experience.

The journey south commenced with a rapid recall from leave, a hasty embarkation in HMS *Invincible* and a most remarkable and moving departure from Portsmouth harbour. The townspeople gave the task force an emotional send-off which was to sustain and encourage us throughout the weeks of tension and action that lay ahead.

Within the squadron we were already delighted with the performance of our aircraft in peacetime and were very keen to get to grips with the enemy. Morale was high and we were glad to be part of the *Invincible* air group. Our association with the ship and our sister squadron, 820 Naval Air Squadron, equipped with Sea Kings, since our first embarkation in early 1981, had been a very happy and rewarding one. We had been tuned to operate as a single entity; with Sea Harriers and Sea Kings acting as flexible extensions of the Captain's will to defend his ship. 1981 had been a good year for all and a very busy one; the high points were Exercises Ocean Safari and Ocean Venture, followed by a squadron fighter combat detachment to Decimomannu in Sardinia. The ship had received high praise for its success in these exercises and the squadron pilots had become expert in the handling of their aircraft and its weapon systems.

At Decimomannu, our team had achieved an overwhelming success rate against the best fighters of the US Air Force (the F15 Eagle and the F5E Aggressors) and this gave us great confidence for the battles to come. Throughout Sea Harrier's time in service, it has never failed to demonstrate that it is one of the best dog-fighting aircraft in the world today. It is far superior in this regime to any other fighter in the UK inventory and more than matches the best of the US Navy and US Air Force.

As the ship progressed southwards, much effort was expended in the fine tuning of both weapon systems and operators. By May 1 we were ready for action in every sense, had great confidence and were more than a little grateful for our earlier exposure to North Atlantic gales. This latter experience had prepared us well for the unpredictable and occasionally vicious weather of the Roaring Forties.

The first day of action began with a combined attack on Port Stanley airfield. Royal Navy frigates and destroyers pounded the defences with naval gunfire support; Sea Harriers from *Hermes* carried out a low-level dawn attack on airfield facilities; and a Vulcan bomber flew from Ascension to attack the runway with bombs before first light.

My own squadron had prepared for a night strike on the airfield and were fully worked up to carry it out. However, our most valuable strength lay in our air intercept expertise, having carried out the full operational trials of the aircraft's radar and weapon system. We therefore launched before the arrival of the Vulcan to protect it and the subsequent *Hermes* Sea Harrier attack from harassment by enemy fighters.

The combined action went very smoothly with our warships and *Hermes'* Sea Harriers on target and the Vulcan achieving slight damage to the runway. The Vulcan's exceptional flight may not have denied the Argentines the use of the runway but it undoubtedly resulted in some enemy casualties and showed the world that we would go to extraordinary lengths to defend our territory.

During the daylight hours of May 1, the first air-to-air actions of

HMS Invincible.

the war took place. It was a most significant day's experience for us all; one in which we became battle-hardened and which left an indelible impression on the Argentine Air Force pilots. Our first real contact with the enemy was when Lieutenant Commander Robin Kent and Lieutenant Brian Haigh engaged a pair of Mirage IIIs north of the islands. The Mirages fired two missiles with apparently more hope than expertise and the Sea Harrier pair were left unscathed. There is little point in firing a missile unless one is sure it is going to achieve the aim. A good fire solution is always necessary and this can only be realised when the aircraft is flown professionally and with total commitment to the fight.

Later that morning, further enemy Mirages were engaged by a second *Invincible* pair led by Lieutenant Commander John Eyton-Jones. The Sea Harriers gave chase to the enemy over East Falkland but received so much ground fire from nearby Argentine ground defences that they were forced to turn away. Apparently it was rather a pleasant firework display until the adrenalin took over!

My own first exposure to the enemy came at about midday when on combat air patrol close to Port Stanley airfield. My number two for this mission was Lieutenant 'Soapy' Watson, fresh from Sea Harrier training but already a most professional operator. The day was beautifully clear with about half-cover of cloud over the island coastline between 800 and 2,500 ft. Our job was to protect a small group of our warships just north of the island (East Falkland) and excitement ran high in the cockpit when our control ship, HMS *Glamorgan,* reported three small aircraft contacts taking off from the runway at Port Stanley – so much for our hopes that the Vulcan raid had been successful!

We were about 20 nautical miles from Stanley, turned towards it and began a rapid descent. Soapy immediately 'taught his grandad new tricks' and acquired the enemy on radar close to the coast and heading north. We continued to close, penetrated the cloud cover and found three startled T34s just on the bottom edge of cloud. They had seen us and immediately nosed up into the cloud, but not before we were close enough to take a longish-range potshot with guns. I pulled through the cloud in chase, passed too close for comfort to one T34 and inverted to pull down below cloud again. They too emerged below but in complete disarray and, most importantly, jettisoning all their bombs and stores into the sea. Part of our aim was therefore achieved and our surface ships were safe.

But at the time I was pretty disgusted with myself for missing with my initial cannon-burst and spent the next two minutes trying to engage the enemy once more as they darted in and out and through the clouds towards the coastline. They used the cloud well, survived and my frustration was complete when I turned for safety as the last T34 disappeared over the well-defended ridge just to the north of the airfield.

Back on patrol together at medium altitude, we had little time for reflection. Three Mirages were reported to the south – approximately 40 miles and closing. Each time we vectored towards them they turned away and so we decided to try to 'spoof' them into combat. We flew north at a leisurely speed and medium altitude. Immediately *Glamorgan's* commentary indicated that they had fallen for the spoof and had begun to close very rapidly. With the bait taken and the enemy 15 miles astern, we turned hard into them and searched our radar screens avidly.

Almost immediately three smoke trails appeared high in the sky ahead, coming directly towards us. Forsaking the radar, I attempted a visual missile lock onto the left-hand trail, and with a mixture of frustration and amusement realised my mistake – I was trying to track an air-to-air-missile! Fortunately it ran out of steam before impact and oscillated its way to the sea below as did the other two missiles. The Mirages had turned for home. It seemed as though the Argentine pilots had no desire to let us get to grips in close and this was causing them to fire beyond the maximum effective range of their missiles.

Having landed safely on board, I continued to feel frustrated even though the mission had taught me much. The aim of the game was to shoot down aircraft and I felt I had missed a chance. For the first time in years I sweated through nightmares (of missed targets) for the next three nights.

As the day progressed, the mood of the squadron and the ship began to change. Frustration was in danger of becoming the order of the day and this was well exemplified by comments to aircrew before getting airborne. On the first mission it had been, 'Goodbye, Boss': by the third mission it was, 'Don't come back without a kill, Boss!' (All in good humour, of course.) The source of this ribaldry was our team of squadron engineers led by Lieutenant Commander Dick Goodenough. These experts in the art of aircraft maintenance were the strong foundation for all our efforts during the conflict. Their outstanding hard work which was based on the highest professional standards ensured that the command had 801's Sea Harriers available for over 99 per cent of all missions tasked. This performance was justly rewarded when Dick was later awarded the MBE.

Gathering gloom broke into brightest day when in mid-afternoon, Lieutenant Steve Thomas and Flight Lieutenant Paul Barton engaged two Mirages at close range. Steve (who generally looked after me as my wingman during the war) used his radar to control the Sea Harriers into firing positions and drew the enemy's fire. Two missiles passed over his cockpit! Meanwhile Paul had achieved a firing solution, released the first Sidewinder AIM-9L of the war and his Mirage target exploded into a ball of flame. Steve fired at the second Mirage which by then was evading towards the clouds below. The missile closed on its target as the aircraft entered cloud and there was no way of knowing whether the kill had been achieved or not.

Morale on board immediately soared and within the squadron it knew no bounds. The Sea Harrier weapon system had come of age, had worked perfectly and had begun to justify our peacetime confidence.

Shortly afterwards, as dusk was falling an even more impressive engagement took place. Lieutenant Alan Curtis and Lieutenant Commander Mike Broadwater, working with our squadron fighter controller, Lieutenant Bob Holmes, intercepted three Canberra aircraft which were inbound to strike the fleet. The enemy aircraft had approached at high level and then descended to low level some 100 miles from the task force. Ship's radar contact with the Canberras had been lost leaving Alan the task of carrying out an autonomous interception in classic style. Using his radar to good advantage, he controlled his pair into a good firing position at very low level below cloud and destroyed the lead aircraft with Sidewinder. Mike fired at the second Canberra (which was by this time making fast tracks for home) and his target was reported to have

A Sea Harrier secured aboard HMS Invincible *is checked by deck crew prior to launch for CAP.*

crashed into the sea before it could limp its way back to the mainland.

The first day of conflict was therefore concluded in style and *Hermes* put the icing on the cake with her first Sea Harrier kill: another Mirage. Although some celebration was in order, the night task remained – pilots on deck alert, in the cockpit, waiting for a new threat to emerge.

The events of May 1 had obviously given the Argentine command food for thought. Sea Harriers had claimed three certain kills and two probables in a variety of tactical situations. It is likely that the Canberra kills, in particular, caused the enemy greatest concern because only one of their aircraft returned home and their pilot's post-flight debrief must have caused some dismay; the Sea Harrier intercept had not been easy but had borne much fruit.

Between May 1 and May 21 there were no further air-to-air actions. The Argentines avoided Sea Harrier like the plague and conserved their assets for the day the task force mounted its invasion. Our squadron was kept very busy, however: airborne throughout the daylight hours, on deck alert and flying by night, providing air defence, bombing the airfield at Port Stanley by day and night and protecting the remaining four Vulcan flights from attack. Without the support of the Sea Harrier over Port Stanley, the final two Vulcan missions could not have taken place.

Most tragically we suffered the loss of Lieutenant Commander John Eyton-Jones and Lieutenant Alan Curtis during this period. They were lost during a patrol mission in bad weather over the sea and in defence of the task force. Their companionship, experience and expertise was sorely missed during the ensuing period, as aircrew fatigue set in and tasked flying remained the same. However, morale recovered rapidly and our engineers continued to work their miracles with the reduced number of aircraft available.

On May 18, the SS *Atlantic Conveyor* rendezvoused with the task force and elements of the newly formed 809 Squadron embarked in *Invincible* and *Hermes*. The four Sea Harriers and their pilots arriving in *Invincible* were a most welcome and much needed reinforcement for the squadron.

May 21 was Argentine Navy Day and the day that the task force established the beach-head in San Carlos Water. It was also the day which saw the hardest-fought and most critical naval and naval air actions of the whole campaign, the battle for Falkland Sound.

Under cover of darkness on the night of May 20–21, the amphibious group entered San Carlos Water and began to disembark 4,000 Royal Marines, soldiers and stores of all descriptions. This mammoth task was to last all day and it was essential for both ships and personnel to be protected from loss. Commodore Mike Clapp, CB, achieved this protection in two ways. In a brilliant tactical move he stationed seven of Her Majesty's warships outside

A Sea Harrier caught by the camera just at exit from the ski-jump launch ramp.

San Carlos Water in the more open reaches of Falkland Sound. These frigates and destroyers were to form the second line of defence against the expected Argentine Air Force onslaught, the first line of defence being provided by Sea Harrier CAPs.

The battle raged throughout daylight hours over and around the Sound. Approximately 70 fighters and fighter bombers (Mirages and Skyhawks) penetrated the Sound to do battle and many more than this number were turned away by the Sea Harrier cordon. An A4 Skyhawk pilot who was shot down in the area shortly after May 21 commented that he and his formation had been turned back on four separate occasions by Sea Harriers before eventually breaking through to attack the amphibious force (out of the frying pan into the fire).

At the end of the day an on-the-spot assessment indicated that the Argentine Air Force had lost 12 Mirages/Skyhawks, two Pucaras, one Chinook and two Pumas. Our losses consisted of one RAF Harrier and two Gazelles plus varying degrees of damage to HMS *Ardent,* (which was later to sink) *Argonaut, Antrim,*

HMS Ardent, *severely damaged at the stern after the Argentine bombing raid.*

Broadsword and *Brilliant. Plymouth* and *Yarmouth* were left unscathed. However there were only four minor casualties to our amphibious troops and the all important aim of protecting the landing had been achieved. No Sea Harriers were lost and these Fleet Air Arm jets manned predominantly by Royal Navy pilots, claimed most of the day's kills.

A considerable volume of uneducated comment has been made concerning the Sea Harrier's achievements in combat during this and other days of action. Much of the veiled or inferred criticism published in the press, particularly by the French, has been in error. Both envy and commercial competitiveness appear to have played a part in such criticism. One frequent comment has been that the enemy aircraft had too little fuel to remain in the target area for more than a few minutes. This was obviously not the case as any student of Mirage and A4 Skyhawk performance figures can easily establish. They had almost as much loiter time available over the target as did the Sea Harrier and, most importantly, they had the considerable advantage of being on the offensive and with vastly superior numbers. A further frequent comment has been that the attacking aircraft had no air-to-air weapons with which to fight. Having been on the receiving end of a Mirage's missile during the afternoon of May 21, I can assure such detractors of the Sea Harrier's achievements that they have 'got it all wrong'. Further, it is worthy of note that following May 21 (and with May 1 in mind), the Argentines christened Sea Harrier the 'Black Death' (*La Muerte Negra*) and publicised this fact on their national radio broadcasts. They lived in fear of the Fleet Air Arm, though to their credit they continued with their almost suicidal offensive against our land and naval forces until Stanley fell.

37

Steve Thomas and I had a particularly good day on May 21. We worked under the control of Lieutenant Commander Lea Hulme who co-ordinated the Sea Harrier efforts against incoming raids from his operations room in HMS *Brilliant.* He gave a tireless and invaluable service and established a strong rapport with my team. Through his information and comment we were able to begin to understand and appreciate the pressure being suffered by the ships in the Sound, and at the same time began to understand that those ships' crews were literally fighting for their lives in a relatively indefensible stretch of water.

The high morale and fighting spirit of our sailors was a tonic to us all, especially when *Brilliant*'s operations room was hit by cannon shells from Mirages: in spite of the mayhem all around, Lieutenant Commander Hulme never faltered but kept his important commentary flowing.

That commentary brought me my first kill when Steve Thomas, Lieutenant Commander Alistair Craig and I were vectored over the land near Goose Green to investigate a slow-moving contact. It turned out to be a Pucara which had been menacing our escorts in the Sound, and it did not take too long to destroy it with cannon fire. Nevertheless the pilot 'stayed with it' gallantly for as long as survival permitted and, having done everything possible to defend himself, finally ejected just before his aircraft impacted the ground. I found out that his name was Major Tomba and that he was the leader of 'Toucan' flight of Pucaras based at Goose Green. He was later to prove a most helpful interpreter for our medics during their treatment of the many Argentine casualties. Later in the day, Steve and I were once more in action against three Mirages at low level over West Falkland. This was the occasion that I mentioned earlier, when one of the Mirages fired a missile at me just before we passed each other canopy to canopy. In the short engagement that followed, Steve achieved one kill and one probable kill and I claimed the third Mirage. Steve's pilot ejected and survived but mine wasn't so lucky.

There was no time to celebrate, however, because we sighted three Skyhawks on the way down the Sound and gave chase. They were too far ahead for us to catch them before they reached the now smoking HMS *Ardent,* but a pair of Sea Harriers from *Hermes* was on hand and knocked two of them down. At this stage I thought I had lost Steve. I couldn't see him or talk to him and searched in vain for signs of a crash on the ground that we had just flown over. It was an awful moment when I felt that he must have been lost. To my immense relief and delight I found him safe and sound when I recovered to the ship – he had been hit by enemy ground fire and had lost his radio. We both had a couple of beers that evening.

From May 21 to the end of the confrontation, there was little time for reflection as each day brought fresh challenges. Our Sea Harriers were in demand on all fronts: defending the beach-head, patrolling the islands, protecting the task force, probing towards

Argentine airspace. It was a most rewarding period for us all and occasionally pretty exciting.

On the day that the *Atlantic Conveyor* was struck by Exocet, I was very fortunate in being on *Invincible*'s deck where I could feel a real part of a mighty warship in action. As I sat in my aircraft not far from the Sea Dart launcher I was given a grandstand view of the war at sea: missiles being launched against the enemy aircraft, *Atlantic Conveyor* smoking from missile impact on the port bow, helicopters and Sea Harriers surrounding the task force. Mine was the only Sea Harrier still in the ship, the remainder having been scrambled; but I was glad to remain there for once and watch my captain and his team defend our ship so well.

Perhaps the last day of particular note for me and worthy of mention here was June 1. It provided my third and final kill of the war which again was achieved with no little help from our surface escorts inshore. Steve and I were climbing out from the San Carlos area en route to 'mother' (HMS *Invincible*) when HMS *Minerva* reported a fleeting contact away to the north-west. *Minerva* was very confident that it could be an air target for us and so we turned from the way home to take a look. My radar screen immediately showed a good solid contact and, with not a little concern for our low fuel state, we set off in pursuit.

In shore, *Minerva* rapidly arranged two decks to take us within San Carlos Water should we be unable to make the long transit home after intercept. The radar contact was soon heading west as fast as it could and hiding below low cloud. Descending through the cloud I was elated to find an enemy Hercules, just a few miles ahead. Time was short for fuel was low, and so, in very quick time, I released both missiles and fired all my gun ammunition into the enemy aircraft. It gracefully dropped its right wing and, on fire, nose-dived into the sea. Downing that aircraft gave us all great satisfaction because the Argentine Hercules pilots had run through our blockade round the islands frequently. They were a most professional team and had resupplied the enemy forces at Stanley and elsewhere with vital munitions on a fairly regular basis.

Our joy at that success (and our safe return on board) was soon dampened that day when one of our planes went missing. Flight Lieutenant Ian Mortimer, the squadron air warfare instructor, was shot down by a surface-to-air-missile near Stanley airfield. He was in his dinghy close to the enemy-held shore and night was falling fast. His precise position was not known and the ship immediately mounted a full-scale helicopter search for him. The 820 Squadron command team of Ralph Wykes-Sneyd, Keith Dudley and Peter Galloway conducted a superb search and rescue operation which eventually culminated in Ian being snatched from under the enemy's noses after nine hours survival in a freezing sea. We celebrated his return with vigour.

It would be wrong to conclude this short account without paying a strong tribute to some of the as yet relatively unsung heroes of the conflict, without whom we could not have carried out our tasks in the air. The submarine fleet were first on the scene of action and they blockaded the Argentine naval ports so successfully that, apart from the *General Belgrano,* the enemy's surface warships were never to trouble us throughout the conflict. This achievement contributed immeasurably towards giving safe passage to our amphibious force en route to San Carlos Water and we owe the Royal Navy submariners a great debt for it. Their success did much to guarantee that our two carriers, *Invincible* and *Hermes,* remained unscathed and that we 'stovies' always had a welcome deck to return to.

My second and final tribute goes to every man serving in the task force surface units. They fed us, supported us steadfastly in every department, encouraged us and protected us. Most of all, however, they gave us pride in our surface fleet, that element of our service without which the Navy could not exist. The final success of the task force deployment lay in their hands and is, in the main, their achievement and our reward.

Commander
Tim Gedge AFC, RN

As a Lieutenant Commander Tim Gedge was commanding officer of 809 Naval Air Squadron during the Falklands campaign. The squadron was re-formed on the commencement of hostilities and has since been disbanded. Appropriately enough, the squadron's badge is that of a Phoenix rising from the flames. Commander Gedge (39), married with three children, joined the Royal Navy in 1963. His first carrier-borne-aircraft flying was in Sea Vixens from HMS *Victorious* in the Far East, after which he went on to fly Hunters as a qualified flying instructor. He moved on to the F4 Phantom in 892 Squadron in 1969 from HMS *Ark Royal* before further training to become an air warfare instructor. He returned to Phantoms, becoming senior pilot of 892 Squadron, and then went on to the staff of Britannia Royal Naval College at Dartmouth. After that followed two years with the Royal Marines as brigade aviation officer, providing advice and liaison between all arms of the services.

It was after his appointment with the Royal Marines that he moved back to full-time flying in 1979, this time to the Sea Harrier, and became Commanding Officer of the first frontline Sea Harrier unit, 800 Naval Air Squadron. He remained CO until early in 1982, when he handed over to Lieutenant Commander Andy Auld. Commander Gedge moved to another Staff appointment, but at the commencement of the Falklands crisis in April 1982 he became heavily involved in the problems of getting the carriers and other ships ready for deployment to the South Atlantic.

Having watched the carriers sail southwards from Portsmouth on April 5, I was contacted by the Flag Officer Naval Air Command's staff at Yeovilton and asked to form another frontline Sea Harrier squadron. Initially the task was to recommence the training pipeline and also to provide a reserve of pilots and aircraft for the South Atlantic operation.

On April 6 I arrived at Yeovilton and began to set about the complicated task of raising a squadron of ten aircraft – twice the size of the normal peacetime Sea Harrier unit. It posed many problems at first, not the least being the question of where to get the aircraft from and how to ensure that they would be fully equipped and ready for war. In addition there was the major question of who would fly them. Sea Harrier pilots were few in number and also spread far and wide. Those on exchange appointments in the United States and Australia were immediately brought home;

others within the United Kingdom were brought back to Yeovilton.

The aircraft that were available were in several stages of refit, repair or still in build at the factory. Once we had managed to get them speeded through their work programmes, and get very early deliveries from British Aerospace, who managed to deliver aircraft well ahead of schedule, we began to consider what colour the paint scheme should be. We knew already that the squadrons at sea in *Hermes* and *Invincible* had repainted their aircraft, but beyond that we were treading new ground.

It was at this stage that we brought in an expert from Royal Aircraft Establishment, Farnborough who had investigated the typical weather conditions of the Falklands area for that time of year and advised us to paint the aircraft in a colour that would blend with that part of the world, light grey. It is interesting to note that the final colour adopted by the Fleet Air Arm for their Sea Harriers after the Falklands campaign is slightly darker than the one we chose and a slightly lighter grey than the one they painted the aircraft while going south in the carriers.

During the ensuing three weeks, a colossal amount of work was done, including getting the aircraft together. The Sea Harriers obviously had to be totally complete for war and the equipment acquisition problems were enormous. It was an incredible effort not only from within the service but from industry as well. Finally, on April 30, we were ready, with eight fully equipped Sea Harriers of 809 Squadron – it was short of the number I had wanted, but we had to leave two behind to form the nucleus of a training programme at Yeovilton. Whatever was happening to the frontline squadrons down south, it was important to continue training and development as far as possible.

We also experienced some difficulty in obtaining the required number of pilots for the eight aircraft. There were six RN pilots but we still had two more to find and had exhausted all RN sources, with the exception of those that were to stay behind and continue the task at home. The solution that we devised was to look for two current RAF Harrier pilots who had Lightning interceptor experience. That would provide us with the best option for a very quick conversion. Fortunately we found them quickly: both were flying with the Harrier squadrons in West Germany and were posted rapidly to Yeovilton. During the next few days they were converted to the Sea Harrier, trained in our tactics, given some ski-jump launch experience at Yeovilton, where there is an adjustable ramp, and also taught how to use the Sea Harrier's radar – quite a daunting task for them and one which they both attacked, achieving creditable results.

At last we got our orders to move – to ferry the aircraft to Ascension Island, using in-flight refuelling. We were to do this in three separate flights over a two-day period.

I departed on the morning of Friday, April 31, with two forma-

The Sea Harriers of 809 Squadron during a UK practice sortie just prior to their flight to Ascension. The aircraft are painted in a lighter grey than their counterparts in the other squadrons already in the South Atlantic.

tions of three aircraft departing at a one-hour interval. The third flight of the remaining two aircraft left Yeovilton on the following day. My group arrived in Ascension on May 1 as did the second wave of three, while the third group arrived a day later. All aircraft refuelled a total of 14 times from RAF Victor tankers during the nine-and-a-quarter-hour flight. The refuelling usually took the form of tanking two aircraft first and then the third. All the tanking went remarkably well and no problems were encountered despite this being the first time that most of us had in-flight refuelled the Sea Harrier.

At Ascension we waited for a few days and it was during this period that the Vulcan carried out the first of the long bombing sorties from Ascension to Port Stanley airfield. We stayed in very rudimentary accommodation at a place called Two Boats Settlement which was located halfway up Green Mountain. Work on the aircraft was kept to a minimum because of the constant volcanic grit and sand blown across the moon-like surface of the island. As soon as we could we covered all the holes and cavities of the aircraft with tape and polythene sheeting to try and stop this grit becoming a problem.

At last, and somewhat thankfully, we left Ascension Island, on May 5. The *Atlantic Conveyor* was anchored a little way off the coast and we flew a short sortie from Wideawake airfield before recovering vertically onto the temporarily fitted vertical landing pad in the forward section of the ship. Aircraft were then parked between the two rows of two-high containers and locked to the outer edges of the deck. These later provided some protection for the air-

craft – without them, the Harriers and helicopters would have been exposed totally to the elements.

We were very conscious of the need to keep the aircraft in pristine condition, and though we washed them thoroughly at Ascension before our short hop they were again given a good washing once aboard *Atlantic Conveyor*. With us were 6 RAF Harrier GR3s which had also tanked out from the United Kingdom, 4 Chinook and 6 Wessex helicopters.

Once aboard, most of the aircraft were covered with purpose-made rubberised canvas bags. One Sea Harrier was kept permanently on alert, fuelled, armed and ready to be launched in the event of the ship being intercepted by an Argentine aircraft. A second Sea Harrier was kept as a back-up. As it turned out, the passage south was uneventful from Ascension to the total exclusion zone around the Falkland Islands.

While on passage – it took 12 days to reach the task force – we carried out some minor work on the aircraft including completing the new radio installations. The most was made of these non-flying days by holding in-depth discussions and briefings on the tactics we would use and which we knew would figure in our future operations. The opportunity was taken to get to know the pilots of No. 1

(F) Squadron and joint briefings were held. Most of them were travelling aboard the North Sea ferry *Norland,* which was sailing in company with *Atlantic Conveyor,* and they transferred over to us on occasion by helicopter.

On May 19 we began transferring the Harriers from *Atlantic Conveyor* to the carriers. Four of 809 Squadron's aircraft were to operate from HMS *Hermes* and four from HMS *Invincible.* I was part of the group aboard *Invincible.* On that particular day, *Hermes* was close to *Atlantic Conveyor,* and *Invincible* was much further away. She was in effect out of range from a vertical take-off launch so I had to fly to *Hermes,* where I refuelled and launched for the longer flight to the deck of *Invincible.* All the RAF GR3s were taken aboard *Hermes.*

By the time it was my turn to launch from *Atlantic Conveyor,* it was coming on to evening, and when I landed on *Hermes* it was virtually dusk. After refuelling and by the time I came to launch, it was nearly dark and it was pitch black when I arrived over *Invincible.* This was a particularly interesting flight for me as it was my first for two weeks and was the first proper night landing I had done for some time. Fortunately during the preparation stages in the United Kingdom, when the squadron was forming, I had flown the Sea Harrier simulator at Yeovilton so the procedures for a night landing were reasonably familiar.

For the next three weeks, until the day of the *Sir Galahad* tragedy, I was in *Invincible,* flying a variety of missions, mainly combat air patrol around the San Carlos area. During this period I also did some ground attack/straffing and a night attack against Argentine positions on Pebble Island. In this we were using Lepus flares at night to illuminate the target areas. On the whole, however, we concentrated on CAP and on playing our part in the air defence battle. The terrain is very similar to that of the western Highlands of Scotland and it was almost a case of *déjà-vu.* I had

Aboard Atlantic Conveyor, *a Sidewinder-armed Sea Harrier was kept ready for launch and interception during the journey from Ascension to the task force.*

often 'fought' Hunters at low level in Scotland and chasing Mirages and Skyhawk A4s over the terrain of West Falkland was remarkably similar.

I think most of us owe our success and indeed our survival to the training we had all undergone. It was of enormous satisfaction to know that we had achieved the right sort of balance in this training. Much of the flying in the South Atlantic was done at extremely low levels and I was very surprised by the lack of coherent tactics displayed by the Argentine Air Force pilots. They were not going about air combat as we would have done and they made some very bad mistakes. Naturally, as soon as this became obvious to us, it boosted our confidence no end – here was the proof that we had been on the right track and our tactics, training and past experience all seemed to drop happily into place. Coupled with that, the aircraft worked and went on working all the time. It was a good combination of trained pilot and machine.

But while I can now sit somewhat dispassionately and analyse our training and the performance of our equipment, and so on, one of the things that really sticks in the mind is the horrific sight of a ship burning, a vessel literally dying before one's eyes. *Sir Galahad* will remain in my memory, burning furiously with lifeboats around her and helicopters reaching in towards the thick smoke, trying to get the survivors out of harm's way. Looking down from a Sea Harrier cockpit, knowing something of what was happening and not being able to do anything positive to help was a bad experience.

Other things I seem to single out mentally are the spectacular sights of aircraft exploding, especially when hit in mid-air at about dusk. The sudden violent balls of flame were bigger explosions that I had expected. The memory of the weather conditions too will remain with me. At times they were quite appalling, and we were attempting to intercept incoming raids at low level in these terrible conditions. It was hard at times to avoid being drawn away from the right area and then to have insufficient fuel for the return to the ship. Also (and quite contrary to the beliefs of the media and later propaganda), we operated at extreme ranges from the carriers, and it was quite something to judge one's fuel state to do the task and then still have enough to return home and recover with only just enough to provide the minimum of safety margin. Happily everyone got the formula right every time and not one aircraft was lost from this cause.

Only the Harrier could, and did, operate under these conditions. Although four Sea Harriers were lost, probably due to the weather and sea state, we were operating in appalling conditions well outside our normal peacetime prescribed limits – by day and often by night too.

To evaluate the overall scene: from the Royal Navy's point of view the operation was a total success. Our aircraft were doing more than we had originally intended – for instance in air defence

A close-up view of the bomb damage of the LSL Sir Tristram *while she is alongside the government jetty in Stanley. At this time, parts of the ship were being used for accommodation until her return to the UK for repair and refit.*

operations against fast attack aircraft. This role was not a specified original requirement for the Sea Harrier, but the flexibility of the aircraft allowed us to take it in our stride. It was so gratifying to see it all work out so well. If it had not, we would almost certainly have lost far more ships and men. Without any air cover, the amphibious landing at San Carlos might well have ended differently.

On June 8, I was sent ashore by Admiral Woodward to operate with the ground forces in order to facilitate the closer working of the combined operations. I had an interesting journey ashore – one-and-a-half hours in a Sea King helicopter at night, followed by being winched down to the deck of the Royal Fleet Auxiliary *Sir Bedevere.* I remained aboard for the next 20 hours while she steamed confidently into San Carlos Water in a fog that I can only describe as being a 'real pea-souper'. When almost in the anchorage this bank of fog suddenly rolled back and we found ourselves right in the middle of the assault force in San Carlos Water. I spent the next seven days in HMS *Fearless,* mainly assisting in the tasking and organisation of the Harrier ground attack missions.

During this period I flew up to Mount Kent, to the Headquarters of 3 Brigade, to talk to them and then went on by light helicopter to Fitzroy Settlement which overlooked the scene where *Sir Galahad* was still burning. This was a totally new aspect of war. Up until now my contact with it had been distant and impersonal. Now I could actually see the enemy himself, in the form of prisoners of war, see the foreign uniforms, hear a different language, listen to the sound of the guns in the distance and see lines of tracer being fired at me. Again, I found it fascinating although somewhat horrific. Walking up through Fitzroy on a clear morning, I was going through the light snow when I stopped to watch a helicopter with wounded aboard. The first thing that occurred to me was how similar it was to the television programme, MASH. The doors of

47

the village hall which served as the medical centre burst open and the medics poured out to help these very badly wounded men. I think that this was the first time that I had ever seen badly wounded men. It was nothing at all like MASH.

On June 14, I was sitting at one of the control desks in *Fearless* – most of my work had been done – and listening to the reports being made over the radio. I heard the first reports coming in of the surrender. The first white flag was seen to fly, even before the last battle was over. From then on, more and more reports came in stating that white flags could be seen. It was rapidly developing into an organisational problem on a massive scale. Strange as it may seem, even transporting the Commander of our land forces, General Moore, into Stanley to accept the surrender was not the easy task one might imagine it to be. With the atrocious weather and the need for a helicopter, it actually proved quite difficult.

A short while later I took a helicopter into Stanley and became involved in setting up the Harrier base on the airfield. We literally had to pace out a suitable length of strip along the runway: not actually the easiest of tasks since there were by now some 5,000 prisoners of war on the airfield peninsula.

Stanley was fascinating, if very depressing. Thousands of prisoners at the airfield, most of them young, all of them cold, dejected and in some cases clearly badly equipped. That sight will also remain fixed in my mind. Stanley itself was an absolute wilderness and littered with high explosives of one kind or another. It was all over the place – small arms ammunition and many other types of weaponry, including Exocet missiles.

The airfield itself has been well chewed up by naval gunfire and bombs – there were craters all around. The Argentines had rigged dummy holes in the runway and I took a close look at one of these. While I was going along the road one day to the airfield, I thought it might be a good idea to have a look at one of their radar units just off the road. Just as I was about to set off to investigate the nearest one, which was only a short distance away, I heard a loud bang further down the road – it was one of our chaps treading on a mine. That put paid to the excursion I had intended. However, my visit did confirm that the Argentine Air Force could have managed limited flights into Stanley at night, using a Hercules on the north side of the runway. It must have been a very hazardous operation to say the least.

Initially there were bodies around but these were very rapidly removed, although a vast amount of refuse remained. The smell was awful. It remained with you all the time and there was no way you could shake it off. In addition the weather was terrible and that just made it worse. I was quite glad to be recalled to *Hermes* from which I was transferred to the tanker, *British Wye*, for the journey back to Ascension. With me were three other pilots, one of whom had travelled south with me in *Atlantic Conveyor*; the other two were from the original 800 Squadron. Also there were 12 of my squadron's maintainers. A total of 22 of us aboard for the journey back.

At Ascension, we transferred to a RAF Hercules for the flight back to Lyneham. It was quite the most uncomfortable flight I think I have ever had. On my return home, I went on leave for a week and then became actively involved with the work-up programme at Yeovilton for the new 809 Squadron, prior to embarking in HMS *Illustrious*. In early August we all boarded this brand new ship and arrived off the Falklands towards the end of the month.

For the next two months, 809 Squadron kept two Sea Harriers permanently ashore at Stanley, alongside the RAF GR3s of No. 1 (F) Squadron, together with three pilots and eight maintainers. We rotated the shore-based personnel every few days to give everyone a fair chance at stretching their legs. While ashore we assisted in the air defence routine of the island, and in addition the RAF flew from time to time from the carrier.

HMS Illustrious *(foreground) finally meets her sister ship HMS* Invincible, *relieving her as principal Falklands guardship.*

It was very interesting to be able to meet the residents of Stanley and some of those from outlying areas, particularly from Goose Green and Darwin. Generally those from the 'camp' – that part of the Falklands outside Stanley – did not journey into town very often as communications were, to put it mildly, difficult. Nevertheless I met quite a large number of the islanders and got quite a good feel for the islands.

By late October the weather had improved greatly and when we left, it was getting even better. The transition from winter to summer took a matter of minutes. The morning we were due to leave there was 2 inches of snow on the ground. By the time we left it was 70 degrees. There is a saying in the Falklands about the changeable weather: 'If you don't like the weather forecast, wait 20 minutes.'

By the time we arrived back in the United Kingdom all of us were pretty much in need of a rest. It had been a most extraordinary year. It was to be my last operational flying appointment and it was my first continuous combat experience in 20 years of almost non-stop flying. In a peculiar way it was most gratifying that these 20 years of flying and simulated war exercises had culminated in a tour of combat duty. I think the most satisfying feature of my flying career was that the training and experience of those 20 years had proved to be right. There was little waste in those years and the naval system had ensured that we were correctly trained when the account was called. We did not fail. We had losses and that's particularly sad for me. But it was not altogether in vain.

Squadron Leader Jerry Pook DFC, RAF

Squadron Leader Jerry Pook was hit by ground fire during a ground attack sortie against Argentinian land forces and was forced to abandon his otherwise largely serviceable Harrier GR3 over the sea when he ran out of fuel, about 35 miles short of the task force. At the time he did not view his chances for survival with much optimism. He was, however, picked up by a Sea King within minutes of hitting the sea and whisked back to his base ship, HMS *Hermes,* flagship of the task force, where he was given the rest of the day off. He experienced no injuries through his ejection and consequently was allowed back quickly to the Squadron's flying strength, taking part in the air attacks on Argentinian positions in the final phase of the fighting. He also had the opportunity of inspecting some the the ground targets once the fighting had ceased.

I flew on the second RAF Harrier ferry flight from the United Kingdom to Ascension Island. We left on May 4 in a formation of four aircraft and on May 6 were on board *Atlantic Conveyor* at Ascension. Arrival on board *Hermes* was on May 18, when we cross-decked via a short VTOL flight to the flagship, which was only a couple of miles away.

On board we had just one day of flying training to become acclimatised to the naval style of operations before we started working on our task in earnest – ground attack and reconnaissance missions in support of the land forces. I flew as the number three on our first operational mission which was an interdiction sortie using cluster bomb units (CBUs), against a large Argentine fuel dump at Fox Bay. I was last man over the target which was burning very well when we had finished with it. The next day was D-Day and before dawn two of us launched from *Hermes* to locate and neutralise an Argentinian helicopter parking area. Following the contours of the hills, we spotted the helicopters and attacked. I was not too lucky on the first pass with CBUs – I missed, but my wingman took out two of them with his 30 mm cannon. I turned back for a second pass and used my cannon to destroy the third. I had attacked in a shallow dive while my wingman was virtually in level flight for his approach. On another occasion I saw and hit a single helicopter on the ground with CBUs, so that made our scores even.

On May 24 it was decided to put on a combined raid on Port Stanley airfield with the RN's Sea Harriers. The idea was to have the Sea Harriers approach over the sea and loft their bombs into the general target area to distract the defenders and keep their heads down, and seconds later for we RAF pilots to come in over the land low and fast to attack the runway. I was not on this particular raid.

The plan worked quite well. Following the Sea Harrier attack, the anti-aircraft artillery was all pointing the other way, in the direction of their approach. The GR3s came in and caught the defences totally unprepared. Once they had dropped their bombs our pilots continued to follow the contours of the ground at ultra low level and maximum speed. A Roland missile was fired after them but fortunately it lost its target signal as the GR3s disappeared behind a hill. I am told another missile was also fired, but that also lost target lock and fell into the sea. On another attack, one of our pilots saw a missile drawing alongside as he left the target area. He jinked to evade it and it exploded outside lethal range.

On May 27, Bob Iveson was hit and successfully ejected as the attack on Goose Green was going on at full tilt. That evening we were asked at very short notice to attack Argentine positions on a peninsula nearby. At that time we were experiencing ordnance shortages as many of our supplies, including CBUs, had been with *Atlantic Conveyor,* which by then had been sunk. Fortunately we were able to use the RN's 2-in rockets as a substitute. I had used SNEB rockets in the past, so my aircraft was fitted with the 2-in rocket pods on the outboard pylons – each one containing 36 rockets.

Firing those weapons was very spectacular. They fired in sequence and there was a continuous burst of flames with pin points of light disappearing down towards the target, followed by a series of explosions. I know it was a case of taking what weapons

Armed with 68 mm SNEB rockets in multi-tube launchers (18 SNEBS per launcher), this GR3 has landed for refuelling at the San Carlos Forward Operating Base.

HSJ – E

we could under the circumstances, but these rockets really were very effective against soft targets.

Another interesting sortie I led was a four-ship formation attack on Goose Green airfield. We approached over land well spread out to produce a less concentrated target for the ground defences, converging at the last minute to hit the target together. This was the first time we had experienced a lot of heavy ground fire – it was well before the Paratroopers had launched their own attack on the area. During the run-in the number three in the formation reported that he was being tracked by radar – a Super Fledermaus serving the Roland surface-to-air-missile system – which did cause us a couple of anxious moments as we knew what would follow. I dropped chaff to confuse the system, while the number three broke away, also dropping chaff. That seemed to work and we escaped unscathed although we saw a lot of heavy anti-aircraft artillery in the target area, a burst of which just missed my aircraft.

As far as the chaff was concerned, we managed to install a temporary arrangement inside the airbrake underneath the rear fuselage. As the airbrake was lowered, the chaff would be released and the enemy radar confused. It worked very well as a temporary fitting, and we later received proper chaff and flare dispensers from the United Kingdom.

The Argentine ground defence firepower was on occasions very heavy, though fortunately not that well directed. It would vary from small arms to 20, 30, 35 and 40 mm guns. It didn't take us very long to gain a great deal of respect for the radar-laid twin 35 mm Oerlikon gun. That proved to be particularly impressive from the receiving end.

I had a chance later, when ashore, to look at the ammunition configuration of those guns; I found that the belt was sequenced with two normal rounds followed by one timed-fused round. The time-fused shells were confusing, as they were intended to be, since they exploded along the trajectory, and could be seen sparkling across the sky. The problem was that the shells would explode at indeterminate intervals along this trajectory which was very off-putting if you were on the receiving end. It was particularly hard to locate the gun that was firing.

Bob Iveson was a friend and valued colleague, so following the Goose Green raid I carried out a solo sortie to search for him. Not that I could have spotted him but I hoped that he would use the personal radio which each pilot carried in his life jacket. I had to break off the search after a time as the Argentinian Air Force were mounting an attack with A4 Skyhawks on the Ajay Bay area. In addition I was very nearly hit by the Argentine defence anti-aircraft artillery, even though I was up at 15,000 ft. I saw some large-calibre tracer passing very close by although I had thought I was out of range.

Argentinian ground forces surrendered to our troops the following day at Goose Green, so we moved our area of operations nearer to Port Stanley as the ring closed around the Islands' capital. Our own troops were being held up by heavy barrage fire from mortar and artillery. It was these weapons that we would now be tasked with neutralising.

It was during these attacks that I had my bad day. En route to the target area, my radio began playing up and went dead for a short time. Fortunately the problem cleared itself for a while just before the attack. I flew through concentrated small arms fire from the ground just before the target and my aircraft was hit. I felt a fairly heavy thump, but everything seemed alright so I carried on with my attack which was on a helicopter landing site. This was deserted, so I flew on to the secondary target, an artillery position about 2 miles away. Coming over a hill, I saw the position in front of me and fired both 2 in rocket pods at it, swamping the area with weapons. It was then I realised that things were not all well. My wingman signalled that I was losing fuel – that must have been the heavy thump earlier.

Just before my radio packed up totally my wingman told me that the fuel loss rate was increasing; by now I also had a hydraulic failure in the No. 1 system. The radio failed again and I felt totally on my own. I decided to try to fly as far as I could towards the carrier so I turned out over the sea and flew in the direction of the task force. But only minutes later I realised that I wouldn't make it. My only hope lay in getting as close to the task force as possible.

The nearest friendly ship was 150 miles away from the Islands and that was a fair amount of flying time when losing fuel at that rate. By now I had climbed and was cruising at about 25,000 ft. Watching the fuel gauge only added to my gloom and left me with one thought: 'How far would I be from the ship on ejection and would I get picked up?' I must admit that at the time I was somewhat gloomy about my chances, flying as I was on my own, with no

(top) An Argentine radar-directed twin 30 mm Oerlikon anti-aircraft gun. This particular gun was positioned on the edge of Port Stanley overlooking the harbour.

(bottom) A 1000 lb Laser Guided Bomb on the outer pylon of a GR3 aboard HMS Hermes.

radio contact and now virtually no fuel. I thought I still had about 100 miles to go.

Suddenly my wingman appeared alongside. That was terrific. He couldn't help, but at least he was there and could act as my radio contact with the ships. Unknown to me, he had been with me all the way and was monitoring my progress and keeping *Hermes* informed. Although I did not know it at the time, *Hermes* herself had acted quickly and had despatched a Sea King to my rescue. After nine or ten minutes flying, the fuel was all gone and the engine died. I waved goodbye to my wingman as I glided towards the sea.

I did not know it at the time, but there was a second Sea King helicopter also in the area. That one was not tasked with my rescue but was flying back to the flagship from another mission – collecting Bob Iveson. Pity, it could have been quite a reunion, the two of us out there in the middle of nowhere.

As I glided down, I prepared myself for the ejection. At 10,000 ft, I pulled the handle and was powered out of the cockpit in a fraction of a second. The chute opened normally and I began my final descent to the sea. In the stillness of the air, I could hear a chopper's rotor blades – relief – it was the Sea King sent out to pick me up.

I hit the water hard and I must admit was not quite prepared for it being so cold. Fortunately I was only in the sea for about ten minutes and was soon being winched up to the comparative safety of the inside of the helicopter. I am entirely grateful to 826 Naval Air Squadron. Not only did they get me out of a nasty situation, but to do so they had to pick me up in 15 ft waves with a 25 knot wind blowing. It wasn't easy, but they managed very well.

Back on board I arrived at the debrief only minutes after my

A typical sight in East Falkland following the Argentine surrender were the large quantities of live ammunition, both cased and loose, lying around.

wingman, who had returned safely. As far as the actual ejection was concerned, it was my first and I hope my last; even though the system worked extremely well it was still quite a rough ride. Like many who eject, I suffered a minor injury – just a stiff neck. I was off flying for only one day before I was ready to fly my next operational mission.

On this next sortie, I flew with the five camera reconnaissance pod on the Harrier's underfuselage pylon. We were trying to locate land-based Exocet missile launchers on which we were now getting a fair amount of intelligence. I searched the Port Stanley area along the coast right up to the airfield, but found nothing. We expected that they would be hard to pinpoint.

My wingman this time flew as decoy – in effect attracting the attention of the defenders but staying out of their range while I came in from another direction to carry out the recce run. It was a complete success; all heads – and guns – were pointing at him, leaving me with a clear run. I came in as low and fast as I could, expecting to pick up a lot of fire from the many guns in the area.

Following that mission we turned our attention to Port Stanley itself although the weather by then was hampering flying operations. I flew two more attack sorties, the first with CBUs on to artillery positions and the second using 'smart' bombs. I released these in a loft attack and they appeared to be very effective, the forward air controller giving me a direct hit on a gun position with the first bomb. With that mission my participation in combat operations came to an end – as did the Falklands fighting shortly after. Even at the time of the surrender we had Harriers in the air, off to attack more targets. They were contacted while en route to the target and were told that white flags were up in Stanley.

Naturally we have thought a lot in retrospect about the campaign in the Falklands. The Ferranti inertial navigation reference and attitude equipment (FINRAE) was, in my opinion, very useful. This equipment was designed to permit inertial alignment to be carried out on the deck of a ship. During our combat operations we found the Argentine flak to be far more effective than their surface-to-air-missile defences. Fortunately for us the Argentinian troops never quite got their act together where small arms fire was concerned. By comparison, the Scots Guards certainly did, bringing down three A4 Skyhawks out of a formation of four on one occasion.

Once ashore we had a good opportunity to look around. We heard from army personnel and civilians that whenever a Harrier or Sea Harrier attacked, a Roland or some other surface-to-air-missile was launched after the retreating aircraft. None of them hit us. Certainly the Argentine forces had plenty of ammunition to spare and that explained the very heavy anti-aircraft artillery fire we experienced. When we subsequently inspected deserted Argentine gun positions, large quantities of ammunition were still lying around ready for use.

As for the Harrier, I can add little to what has already been said about its capabilities. It is after all a very complex aircraft, packed with equipment in a very compact airframe. Any aircraft is vulnerable, of course, but the Harrier proved time and time again, that it could take – as well as give – punishment. The Harriers that were lost to ground fire were hit good and hard before they were brought down. Other Harriers with hits – and some of these were not minor – returned successfully to the ship with very few serious problems, except for one aircraft which was hit in the rear reaction control duct later in the conflict. That aircraft arrived on deck virtually on fire. Certainly it was too hot to go near and the paint in places was burned right down to the bare metal. In spite of this there was no loss of control in the vertical landing and the aircraft was repaired and back flying again within a surprisingly short space of time.

Of course we would have liked armour plate around some areas, but the extra weight would mean that some other item of equipment would have to be discarded – and that wouldn't have been very acceptable either!

During the conflict I had to keep reminding myself that we were operating miles out at sea, launching from a small carrier that bounced around, to carry out ground attacks 250 miles away. The nearest friendly runway lay 3,500 miles away at Ascension Island and the V/STOL Harrier was certainly crucial to the success of this operation. The ability to land on any small strip or ship is the key to the operational flexibility of our tactical airpower in the Falklands. I pitied the Argentine Air Force, diving into the attack not knowing whether or not they would have sufficient fuel to get back to their mainland bases. I am sure many of them did not make it.

Our superiority in training and equipment won the day. In particular, our training in the United Kingdom and Europe in ultra low-level flying proved vital to our operational success. It is a pity that we can't do even more of this type of training in peacetime. As far as ground attack is concerned, no matter how low or fast an aircraft is, it is going to get shot at and hit quite often if it flies anywhere near a defended target.

Lieutenant Commander Andy Auld DSC, RN

Lieutenant Commander Andrew Auld was 800 Squadron's Commanding Officer during the Falklands crisis. He is credited with having shot down two Argentine aircraft and was awarded the Distinguished Service Cross as a result of his actions and the leadership he provided to 800 Squadron. Prior to the introduction of the Sea Harrier in RN service, Andy Auld flew F4 Phantoms from HMS *Ark Royal*.

I think I first got an inkling that we would be going into action when the scrap dealers refused to leave South Georgia. There was still some doubt in my mind but I can remember thinking, 'Is it going to happen?' and 'Will we see some action?' As time went on, some of us realised that we might *have* to go – others thought the political situation would just blow over and the scrap dealers leave the island. It was not to be. Having known some South Americans and judged their character and temperament, I must admit that I thought we would be going into action and for me the invasion of the Falkland Islands made it certain.

As with the other squadron commanding officers, I was called at about 0400 hours on April 2 and told to bring 800 Squadron to immediate readiness. Considering we were due to go on leave at midday, I think we did well to be ready in all respects for embarkation by 1100 hours. Our sister unit, 801 Squadron, was actually on leave so its recall took slightly longer than ours. Fortunately we had rehearsed our call-out several times and it worked very well. While the squadron was made ready to proceed, we still had no 'Charlie' time for embarking.

The bustle and activity at Yeovilton was incredible. I have never witnessed anything like it before, what with all the preparations, and the personnel and the stores that were being organised for delivery to Portsmouth and embarkation.

By 1600 hours, we were embarked in *Hermes* with eight instead of our usual five aircraft. The additional aircraft belonged to 899 Squadron, many of whom embarked with us. For the remainder of the weekend we helped store ship – officers and ratings alike we all joined the long lines of men who were passing tons and tons of stores aboard. Whether food or equipment, it just disappeared into the ship to be stored in any available area. After storing ship to levels suitable to support an extended deployment 8,000 miles away, *Hermes* and *Invincible* sailed with their escorts on Monday, April 5. A further three aircraft embarked during the weekend and the twelfth shortly after sailing.

After we left Portsmouth – and the departure was amazing with the shores black with people all cheering and waving, with banners flying – we settled down to the real work in hand. We all knew we had to 'get up to speed' on the enemy order of battle and get to know the type of equipment that would be ranged against us. Having established that, we then began to investigate the various counter-measures open to us and appointed groups of pilots to look into the areas likely to affect us. These groups reported back to the senior members of the squadron and the discussions were then taken a stage further, to provide a firm base for future training and other actions. The one thing we did find was that our training, even though orientated largely towards the NATO scenario, would stand us in very good stead to meet the threats we were likely to face in any action of the South Atlantic.

Having dealt with the theory, we then set about conducting a flying programme geared towards meeting the requirements of a campaign in the Falklands, to work up a nucleus of experienced pilots and to familiarise the others who had less experience. One of

A deck view of the Sea Harriers of 800 and 899 Squadrons lined up in HMS Hermes just prior to the carrier's departure from Portsmouth. Together with the RN Sea Kings, it made a very cluttered flight deck. In the background, another Sea Harrier approaches the ship for its vertical recovery to the deck.

the younger pilots had been taken from his Sea Harrier conversion course with less than 30 hours on type. Several others although experienced Harrier pilots had just begun their 're-fam' flying.

All the new pilots quickly achieved a satisfactory standard of deck operations and the ship meanwhile worked up to intensive rates of flying operations, typically 40 Sea Harrier sorties per day as well as operating anti-submarine warfare (ASW) routines and drills and flying the helicopters. By the time the task force arrive off Ascension Island, the pilots were in good flying practice in the attack role and had first-hand experience in the practical techniques of rendezvous and transit flying in large formations and in ship attack profiles.

Unfortunately, due to the large amount of air activity at Ascension, we were unable to practice ground attack missions while we were there. Departure from the island was more hasty than intended due to the sighting of what a look-out believed to be a submarine periscope. He was wrong, as it turned out.

Having sailed at action stations, the task force remained on a war footing with Sea Harriers maintaining an around-the-clock alert state. An alert state of one form or another was maintained by the Sea Harriers from that time until we once again reached Ascension on the way home. It was only two days after leaving Ascension on the way south that we made our first contact with the Argentine Air Force Boeing 707 reconnaissance aircraft and this became a daily event as they monitored our steady approach. We maintained a continuous combat air patrol of two aircraft by day and one by night once we reached latitude 35 South.

Each carrier had been allotted its own particular tasks and areas of responsibility. HMS *Invincible* was to provide CAP while we in *Hermes* undertook the ground support role. But it was not quite that clearcut as it turned out later.

We came to the first raid against Port Stanley on May 1. We launched all 12 Sea Harriers from *Hermes* in just under 4 minutes, 9 directed against Port Stanley airfield while the other 3, led by Lieutenant Commander R. Frederiksen, hit Goose Green. For the mission, the aircraft carried a variety of weapons, including cluster bombs and 1,000 lb direct action and air burst bombs. We returned on board to change over to the air defence role, launching the first aircraft less than 30 minutes after landing. We anticipated retaliation, but nothing happened. Hostile aircraft were observed on radar to the west of the task force, but none came further east than over the islands. Later that day events hotted up again and we had our first victory when Flight Lieutenant Bertie Penfold of 899 Squadron, shot down a Mirage. 801 Squadron had already got their first kill that day in which I believe there was a total of 3 engagements, 2 against Mirages and 1 against Canberras. In each of the Mirage engagements, 2 Sea Harriers and 2–3 Mirages were involved, the latter coming down from height releasing their missiles head on at about 5 km range.

All the approaching missiles were successfully evaded by the Sea Harriers, and in the resulting combats 2 Sea Harriers achieved confirmed kills on 2 Mirages. The 3 Canberras encountered had been detected by Blue Fox radar at low level, and were intercepted at between 500 and 1,000 ft. One confirmed kill was achieved and a second Canberra was seen to depart from the area trailing smoke.

After this initial period of frantic activity, events became shrouded in Falklands fog – our first experience of several days of extremely poor visibility. Excitement during these days was provided by the need to operate in minimal weather conditions often with a cloud base as low as 200 ft and visibility at half a mile at the most. In these conditions, pilots were greatly assisted in approaching the ship for landing by the Blue Fox radar, one Sea Harrier actually recovering to the ship with visibility down to 200 metres.

After the first troops were put ashore on May 21, CAPs were established around the landing area, which Sea Harriers were not allowed to enter and where surface weapons could be used freely against any aircraft penetrating this inner defence zone. A factor during the landing phase was the excellent weather and visibility which, while providing super conditions for the landing, also provided good flying conditions for the Argentinians. Naturally, they took full advantage of these conditions and launched a considerable number of attacks. Numerous engagements between Sea Harriers and Pucaras, Skyhawks and Mirages resulted. Harriers were directed on to incoming raids by ships' radar and then made

Two Sea Harriers return at dusk.

visual acquisition. Only a limited number of autonomous Blue Fox detections of low-flying aircraft were achieved. All engagements involved hard manoeuvring, typically 550 knots at 50 to 500 ft. On sighting the Sea Harriers, the Argentines usually jettisoned their fuel tanks and weapons and manoeuvred hard to avoid us. Air combat did not result probably due to the devastating effect of the Sidewinder AIM-9L missiles at low level. In three engagements on May 21, 5 Skyhawk kills were confirmed, 4 with Sidewinder and 1 with guns.

The Argentinians appeared unable to sustain the remarkable opening effort of May 21 and the squadron was involved in only three other engagements, all against Mirage aircraft at low level. In the first clash, 2 Sea Harriers took on 2 Mirages and shot 1 down; in the second, 4 Mirages were intercepted by a pair of our aircraft and 3 were splashed. That was on May 24. Again, on June 8, 2 of our Sea Harriers took on another formation of 4 Mirages and splashed the lot – all of them confirmed. The total *Hermes* bag amounted to 5 Skyhawks and 8 Mirages – all in air-to-air combat – and 2 helicopters and a sizeable number of Pucara attack aircraft shot up on the ground.

I think on reflection, it probably took the task force five or six days of actual action to break the back of the Argentine air attacks. We continued to fly CAPs, but when these were not required, we launched bombing raids on Stanley airfield.

During the phase in support of the landing operations, and indeed throughout the Falklands campaign, Sea Harrier availability was excellent. At least 12 out of 14 aircraft were available each and all day with pilots flying double sorties, remaining in the cockpit between flights and regularly achieving four sorties per day, with often as many as 8 aircraft in the air at any one time from *Hermes* alone. This was in addition to the regular night bombing sorties flown against Stanley.

When the RAF detachment from No. 1 (F) Squadron arrived on board, we were relieved of much of the bombing work. My recollections of their integration into the ship's routine are that it went well and they very quickly settled in. Of course RN and RAF Harrier pilots share the same training – at least in the early stages of conversion to V/STOL – so we were also meeting some old friends. RAF pilots were also on exchange in 800 Squadron, flying Sea Harriers.

An interesting development following the securing of the San Carlos beach-head was the use of the FOB at Port San Carlos adjacent to the landing area. This was an 800 ft aluminium plank strip with refuelling facilities and little else. Harriers launched from *Hermes* for CAP over the island, and as long as weapons were not expended and the aircraft remained serviceable, it could continue to operate on CAP by refuelling at this forward base. Often as many as six Harriers could be found at the FOB at any one time. Pilots encountered no problems in translating from ship

Forced to divert through lack of fuel when the FOB was temporarily unserviceable, a Sea Harrier of 800 Squadron lands aboard the aft platform of HMS Intrepid.

to shore operations and back again. Indeed on one occasion the landing ships HMS *Fearless* and HMS *Intrepid* were used for refuelling purposes. The aircraft landed vertically and took on sufficient fuel from the two ships, enough to get them back to the carrier.

Commenting generally on the squadron and its personnel during the campaign, I would like to say that I am extremely proud of the way everyone performed their duties. And when I say that I am not just talking about the pilots, with whom I work very closely, but also the engineers, technicians and ground crew who together make up 800 Squadron. The maintainers worked 12 hours a day for three months non-stop and there was never any indication of breakdown, either organisational or personal. The conditions under which the men had to work, and work efficiently, were uncomfortable at times, to say the least. It was a crowded ship and the decision to close off No. 5 deck and below for safety reasons meant that the personnel who would have slept there had to squeeze in anywhere they could.

The flight deck crew had to work in temperatures that dropped to freezing, or in a very damp atmosphere with winds across the deck of up to 30 knots, and often in total darkness. The aircraft exceeded all our expectations, and as a complete system, including weapons, the Sea Harrier proved it worked, and in very tough circumstances.

Having returned from the South Atlantic, the squadrons reverted to peacetime strengths and organisation. 899 Headquarters and Training Squadron now have their aircraft back, 809 Squadron, which was raised only for the hostilities, is now disbanded and the two frontline squadrons, 800 and 801, are back to normal. Of the original personnel who went with 800 Squadron down to the South Atlantic, I think I still have about 85 per cent of them with the unit today. As a parting remark about the aircraft, I would say the Sea Harrier is not and cannot be all things to all men, but I consider it the outstanding success story of the Falklands.

Lieutenant Commander Roger Bennett RN

Lieutenant Commander Roger Bennett (34) was Air Engineering Officer of 800 Naval Air Squadron aboard HMS *Hermes* during the campaign. At the end of March 1982, he was due to go on leave for two weeks, but events in the South Atlantic meant that his leave had to be postponed for four months. Married with one child, he is a keen amateur photographer and many pictures in this publication are his work.

Just prior to the events which led up to my unit being sent to the South Atlantic along with other elements of the task force, I had been receiving a number of questions from my senior officers that, if I had thought about them in depth, might have given me a clue that something was in the wind. Questions such as: 'How long would it take to get the squadron to full readiness for war?' and 'How well are we equipped for action in cold climates?' obviously started a train of thought; but all too soon it had happened, and conjecture was replaced by fact. The rude awakening, literally, came at 4.30 a.m. on Friday, April 2, when the phone rang and the duty lieutenant commander told me that the squadron was to come to immediate readiness. I was informed during that call that the squadron might expect to embark with eight Sea Harriers, instead of the usual complement of five, the additional three aircraft to come from 899 Squadron, the Sea Harrier Headquarters and Training unit, also based at Royal Naval Air Station, Yeovilton in Somerset.

My immediate reaction was to have a cup of tea and sit down to collect my thoughts, deciding what needed doing and what were the priorities. Initially, I thought the first move has got to be the personnel recall system which I began to instigate. I called Lieutenant Commander David Chapman, the Air Engineering Officer of 899 Squadron, and my opposite number, to inform him that 800 Squadron would be requiring three of his aircraft and so would the other Sea Harrier operational unit, 801 Squadron, which was to go to HMS *Invincible*.

I had often wondered if the recall system would work. It did, like a charm. It was efficient and quick and by 1100 hours that morning

63

the normal 800 Squadron strength of five aircraft and 100+ men were ready to move. We did not leave immediately, however, and it was not until about 1500 hours that we finally set off, now with the three extra aircraft supplied by 899 Squadron. The Sea Harriers flew direct to HMS *Hermes*, alongside the wall at Portsmouth, while the rest of us piled aboard lorries and coaches for the road journey to the ship.

It was an interesting arrival. *Hermes* was already crowded and the situation seemed chaotic with long lines of lorries arriving and with personnel and stores building up everywhere. The deck carried helicopters, etc., and scaffolding was still in place around the ship's island, erected for dockyard maintenance. Now, in the middle of it all, 800 Squadron needed to land on.

With our eight aircraft on board we settled in quickly and then turned our thoughts and attention to helping load ship. During that particular weekend, the whole of Portsmouth dockyard was seething with activity as lorry load after lorry load of stores and ammunition to cover every eventuality was loaded on to every ship in sight.

Also during that weekend, we had received another three Sea Harriers, bringing our strength up to 11. On Monday, April 5, we sailed. None of us will ever forget the scenes and the emotion. The shores of Southsea lined with thousands of people cheering as the two carriers emerged, their flight decks packed with Sea Harriers and helicopters and all the paraphernalia of war. This proved to be one of the most moving occasions any one of us on board can remember, as no one knew when, or indeed if, we would be coming back. Shortly after leaving Portsmouth, we were joined by the last Sea Harrier bringing our strength, supplemented by 899 Squadron, to 12 aircraft, operated by 16 pilots, 3 air engineering officers and 154 ratings.

As the ship steamed down-Channel to turn south through the Bay of Biscay, it was uncertain whether the ships' company would be seeing action or not, but we worked on the assumption that we would and acted accordingly. Within a fairly short time we had changed our normal duty shifts and were working a two-watch system, 8 hours on and 8 hours off, around the clock 7 days a week.

In spite of the vastly increased workload, a cramped ship and an uncertain situation facing us, morale within 800 Squadron was excellent. The unit worked like a well-oiled machine, there were very few hiccups and if any problem did arise, we all got involved. During the entire campaign, not one case of disciplinary action needed to be taken in the unit.

The work we had to do to the Sea Harriers was varied and ranged from technically demanding tasks such as the fitting of radars to aircraft that had been embarked without them installed to the rather more simple task of painting the aircraft for their war role. On embarkation, all our aircraft were painted in the standard scheme of topside dark grey and underside white and the original five aircraft of 800 Squadron also sported a large and very visible red insignia on the fin. That had to go. If target spotting for the Argentinians was to be made a litle more difficult, camouflage was going to be necessary. In HMS *Invincible,* work was continuing along much the same course, but when it came to painting their aircraft, they had an advantage. *Invincible,* being a newer ship has a very efficient air-conditioning system and the maintenance crews were able to spray-paint the aircraft of 801 Squadron with their new colours. We, on the other hand, were less fortunate as the air-conditioning system in the hanger could not take the consequences of spray-painting, so we had to hand-paint, *and* do some of them on deck as well! The new colour scheme involved painting over the white underside to match the topside. In addition we also painted out the red tail badge and the white part of the roundels to produce the 'mean warlike machine' which became so well publicised by the television team aboard *Hermes.*

Since returning, I have seen aircraft enthusiasts and spotter/modeller magazines make a great point of getting the correct colour for the various aircraft. Our Sea Harriers differed in detail from those of 801 and (later) those of 809 Squadron. In fact what is not realised is that we had no directive as to the precise colour to paint the aircraft and we just picked what we thought would be appropriate, or rather selected the colour we had, most of which happened to be dark grey. It was nevertheless a most effective camouflage.

While we were sorting out the engineering requirements of the squadron's aircraft, the pilot training was also stepped up as several of the aircrew were fairly inexperienced, in that they had

Arming a Sea Harrier with an AIM-9L Sidewinder aboard HMS Hermes *prior to launch for CAP.*

65

only just completed training at Yeovilton. One of them was in fact
only one-third of the way through his Sea Harrier training, which
he completed en route south, and he carried out his first ever ski-
jump launch while we were transiting the Bay of Biscay —out of
range of shore diversion.

Every day saw aircraft launched from the carriers, and during
the first leg of the journey, from the United Kingdom to Ascension
Island, sometimes in excess of 24 sorties were flown each day to
help the squadrons reach peak efficiency. These training missions
were mostly air-to-air combat and ship attack sorties: unfortunately we did not get a chance to try ground attack modes. Our first
taste of *that* role would be 'for real'.

Life aboard *Hermes* was different from our past experiences in
the ship. I would say that during this early period, the flight deck
seemed forever crowded and the handling crews increasingly vir-
tuoso at devising new methods of launching, recovering, manoeuvring and spotting the aircraft on the deck – they had over
twice the number of Sea Harriers they had ever handled before.
Little did we realise that the problems we experienced with 12
would be nothing compared with the 21 Sea Harriers and Harriers
we would have on deck later in May.

While the pilots were practising missions or being trained up to
full combat standard, the Squadron Engineering Department was
also training, putting the deck crews through their drills, speeding
up turnround times and checking weaponry and release circuits,
etc. This support work included the fitting and testing of rocket
pods, practice loading of 1,000 lb bombs and Sidewinder missiles,
and of course re-arming with live 30 mm ammunition for the twin
Aden guns. Loading times and techniques were constantly improved to develop the weapon teams into more efficient groups
which could be guaranteed not to make mistakes when the crunch
came.

In addition, the aircraft's weapon system and the digital compu-
ters were checked with the revised software programmes being
fully evaluated both in the hangar and on deck as well as in the air.
The recently fitted Blue Fox radars – an integral part of the
weapon systems – were checked and adjusted for maximum
performance.

Obviously, while our primary concern was for the aircraft and
the squadron as a fighting unit, we were also part of a much larger
fighting machine, *Hermes* herself. Being part of the ship's complement also demanded our attention in the form of practising action
stations as well as participating in damage control drills, etc. The
concentration of work and exercises increased as we left home
waters further and further behind. We little dreamt of just how uncomfortable life would be and, indeed, how easily we would learn to
cope.

As we neared Ascension Island, 800 Squadron carried out an impressive fire-power demonstration after a dawn launch of ten air-

The Flagship's 'goalkeeper', HMS Broadsword, *armed with Sea Wolf close alongside HMS* Hermes.

(right) *A Wessex helicopter brings aboard additional stores.*

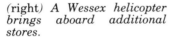

craft, showing visual proof of our work, using all types of live weapons. This included the dropping of bombs, firing of 2 in rockets and the release of a Sidewinder missile using a flare for its target. It was with some relief that we found the weapons worked, particularly as it was all done before television cameras with the results seen on newscasts in the United Kingdom.

It was during this first leg of our 8,000 mile journey that we were joined by our 'goalkeeper', HMS *Broadsword,* a Type 22 frigate, which was equipped with the formidable close-range surface-to-air Sea Wolf missile system. She was to remain with us as our close air defence ship until we were nearly home again some months later.

About two weeks after leaving the United Kingdom, we arrived at Ascension. We had not been steaming particularly hard, I presume to allow the politicians extra time in which to seek a non-violent solution to the Falklands situation. But, as no word of an agreement was forthcoming, the message was being driven home in our minds – we were steaming to war.

When we arrived at Ascension, the normally quiet island was seething with activity involving aircraft, ships, personnel and

67

stores of all kinds. A tented city had sprung up near the large parking apron on the airfield. We remained there at anchor offshore for a few days, taking on board additional stores and it was at this point that Admiral Woodward and his staff were embarked. Final preparations were still being completed when the ship was hurriedly called to action stations. A lookout had spotted a periscope. It turned out to be a false alarm – I believe it was a whale – but the ship was cleared for action, closed up and had weighed anchor in 12 minutes.

As we left the anchorage, *Invincible* came steaming up fast to investigate, but she was not needed. Although it was a false alarm, it gave all of us ample demonstration of how effective our preparations had been. *Hermes'* crew operated at a very high pitch and from that moment on most of us felt we were moving south for a purpose and that conflict was almost inevitable.

Not long after leaving Ascension, we conducted a day-long replenishment at sea when we received supplies of fresh fruit and vegetables. It was to be our last supply for many weeks to come. Our normally deserted weather decks were piled high with sacks of potatoes. Not knowing how long it would be before we could restock, portion control became a byword for accurately measured quantities of adequate but, I hasten to add, uninspiring food – broccoli, sweetcorn and potatoes seemed to form the staple diet.

Moving south, we heard the announcement establishing the total exclusion zone and then we had our first contact with the Argentinians. Shortly after leaving Ascension a Boeing 707 in military markings was detected at long range and intercepted by a Sea Harrier from our ship. Obviously the aircraft was being despatched to check our position, a duty which it carried out faithfully every day. We in turn sent out a Sea Harrier to intercept it. At that time we were told to take no action against the Boeing, though the very day we received orders we could open fire it did not turn up, and we never saw it again. The 707's visits ceased on the day that a small advance task group, led by HMS *Brilliant,* a Type 22 frigate, recaptured South Georgia.

By now the task force was itself nearing the total exclusion zone, and at the end of April it was actually within range of our Sea Harriers. Several Sea Harriers in both *Hermes* and *Invincible* were being maintained on alert 5 (armed, manned and ready to launch within five minutes of a 'scramble'), and two aircraft were on constant combat air patrol ahead of the ship. At this time, all aircraft were fitted with two Sidewinders and carried 200+ rounds of 30 mm high-explosive ammunition in the Aden gun pods.

One point that became apparent fairly quickly with the combat readiness of the Sea Harriers was that when an aircraft on alert 5 was scrambled, the time taken from the order being given to the Harrier launching from the ski-jump was usually about half that required. We often timed alert 5 aircraft launches inside three minutes. If they were ready, they just went.

While air action really got going over the Falklands proper in the early hours of May 1, our tasks on the engineering side actually began much earlier, during the hours from dusk the previous day. We were tasked with preparing the Sea Harriers for their first ever trial by combat, with nine due to attack Stanley airfield and three to be launched at Goose Green. While we armed the 12 aircraft with variously fused 1,000 lb bombs and cluster bombs, the task force was steaming rapidly towards the targets.

Even as we prepared the Sea Harriers for their first taste of combat, an RAF Vulcan was receiving its own baptism of action – at a time when the aircraft was in the process of being withdrawn after a quarter of a century of frontline service. While we launched our 12 Sea Harriers, *Invincible* launched her 8 to provide air cover to counter the expected retaliatory attacks that we felt must follow. All our aircraft therefore had gone.

Along with others, I personally did not expect to see them all return. We had our hearts in our mouths during the raid and we remained at action stations as it seemed the best thing to do. Fortunately all the aircraft returned to both ships. Since then we have often heard the quote from Brian Hanrahan of the BBC who coined the phrase: 'I counted them all out and I counted them all back.' With a total of 20 aircraft in the air taking part in the first offensive action against the Argentine defences, we naturally expected casualties. After all we were at that time not completely aware of the stength and distribution of their defensive forces nor the capability of their anti-aircraft artillery and surface-to-air-missile systems.

Even though the Argentine ground forces were still on the alert after the bombing raid by the lone Vulcan, which had disgorged 21 1,000 lb bombs across Stanley airfield, our Harriers got through with only one being hit. On landing, this aircraft, which had taken part in the attack on Port Stanley, was found to have been hit in the tail fin from anti-aircraft fire. Luckily the shell – possibly a 20 mm – missed the more vulnerable areas.

Within three hours the damage had been repaired and the aircraft was serviceable again. In fact we could have had the aircraft flying again in a much shorter time, but at that point we engineers were still feeling our way with battle damage repairs. Later we proved we could have halved the time at least. At that time we had only one problem, the minor one of persuading our skilled and dedicated airframe artificers that the most important thing to do was to repair the damage and get it serviceable again, not to be over-concerned about the aircraft's looks. I think that says much about the quality of our maintainers, who, even under those conditions, fully expected and were prepared to complete repairs to peacetime standards. We had to concentrate on speed of repair and not exclusively on quality. And when we came across minor routine faults, we tended to mark these in the defects page of the aircraft's logbook and get round to them as and when possible.

Naturally we adopted the fastest route to provide the Commander with the maximum number of aircraft at all times. That was the most important point of all, and to make sure that what he got could do the job.

The other 11 Sea Harriers in *Hermes* and all those from 801 Squadron returned safely. Although everyone was jubilant, there was no time for celebration because even as the aircraft were landing, a red air alert was declared and the rush was on to re-role the Sea Harriers for air defence by fitting Sidewinder air-to-air-missiles, refuelling the aircraft and checking for damage. As soon as they were ready, the aircraft were scrambled on CAP and they left the ship in a constant stream throughout that day.

We achieved a turn-a-round of 20 minutes from the Sea Harriers arriving back aboard to the first pair leaving, armed and ready for air defence. It proved to be one of the most hectic days of the war and we remained at action stations until well after dark. When the task force withdrew to the east, we still had 12 serviceable Sea Harriers. Thereafter of course the pace was slackened off and we would tend to deploy rather less aircraft against a ground target, say four or five, leaving the remainder on board or for the CAP role.

Apart from the first bombing raid, May 1 also brought with it the first 'kill'. An Argentine Mirage was successfully attacked by a Sea Harrier from our squadron and shot down with a Sidewinder. Later that same day, a Mirage and a Canberra fell to 801 Squadron and I believe the Argentine defence forces also scored on one of their Mirages as well, giving a score of 4–0, including the 'own goal'.

It had been a good opening day and morale was running very high. After all we had launched all 12 of our aircraft and recovered them with minor damage to only one. Several Argentine aircraft had been shot down and an unknown amount of damage had been done to the occupying forces on the ground. We felt confident about the future.

Fortunately the night hours were quiet and we made the most of these to carry out routine servicing and the battle damage repairs. The ingenuity with which some of the problems were overcome and the initiative shown by people was marvellous. For example, the weather in the South Atlantic was severe. It was early winter and there was frequently 100 per cent humidity, which caused problems as the aircraft cockpits were literally dripping wet. This in turn affected the integrity of the electrics due to condensation on the cockpit panels and switches, so a cure had to be found. We had tried all sorts of ad hoc remedies until one of our senior rates came up with the idea of using clingfilm to cover a particularly prone display. It worked, as you could still see the digital display through the waterproof film. Some solutions were born out of vague ideas formed by one person who would come up with a suggestion. This would then be discussed among others until it was refined and practical, and then it would be tried.

But damp was really our main problem. Water ingress to the Blue Fox radar located in the Sea Harrier's nose cone also had to be stopped. We discovered the moisture was getting in where the Pitot tube joined the fuselage. We tried a number of fixes and eventually came up with a bath-edge sealing compound from the ship's stores that seemed to do the job.

Water also got into the cockpit itself. That was resolved with the installation of a tonneau cover which directed water away from the electronics. However it was never the rain that caused the problems, but the moisture in the air. We overcame these setbacks rather well and in a very co-operative way. Whenever a problem arose, we could call on the experience of about 160 personnel within the squadron as well as that of an almost equal number of maintainers in *Invincible*. Usually between us we came up with a solution to whatever was the current engineering worry.

I kept in contact with my opposite number, Lieutenant Commander Richard Goodenough in *Invincible*, on almost a daily basis. We used the secure (scrambled) radio-telephone link and discussed problems and possible solutions or reported findings to each other. It was a two-way street of considerable help to both units.

Sometimes in *Hermes* we would end the day with eight or nine aircraft serviceable, but by the following morning all were back on deck and ready, except perhaps for one. All the repairs on deck had to be carried out in freezing cold and in the dark (it was pitch dark), and sometimes in storms as well. Rolling and pitching limits for launching aircraft and moving them about the hangar and flight deck were largely ignored and other rules used for guidance rather than prevention. One of the more gratifying things to us engineers was the much reduced paperwork. The work got done, and what is more no one was ever heard to complain of the rather difficult surroundings or workload.

On May 2 we maintained CAP aircraft throughout the day, but it remained unnervingly quiet, and on the following day we encountered the Falklands fog for the first time. It was an eerie and uncomfortable experience and an uneasy silence descended on us, broken only by the news of the sinking of the *General Belgrano*. During these fog-bound days – and there were many more to come – we maintained the aircraft on alert 5, manned and ready to launch for defence. The pilots would sit in the cockpit, waiting for a couple of hours at a stretch.

With the very poor visibility during those periods, I think the pilots were more than aware of the daunting prospect of landing back on board. It could so easily have been impossible and, if called, they could well have launched on a mission from which they could not have returned without wet feet, if they returned at all.

Every dawn and dusk we went to action stations as standard routine because these times were considered the most likely for an attack. But as the days went by we got to know the Argentines' pattern. They never attacked at dawn, always in the mid or late afternoon and just before dusk.

On May 4, the fog lifted and it turned out a bright clear day as the ships headed west towards the islands. Nice day it might have been, but I could not shake off a feeling of foreboding. It turned out to be right.

At about 14.30 hours all hell broke loose. I was talking to the Commander in FLYCO shortly after lunch when a broadcast from the operations room came through – 'Five bogies at 25 miles. Red air alert.' Within seconds the Commander had rushed to the bridge to sound the action stations hooter that ruled our lives. As its piercing note reverberated through the hull, hundreds of men ran for their action stations.

But before I had even put on my anti-flash gear, which we all had to carry wherever we went, HMS *Sheffield* had been hit by an Exocet launched from an Argentine Navy Super Etendard. Sea Harriers were scrambled, but the Super Etendards made good their escape. While the Sea Harriers were launching in a bid to intercept the attackers, a massive rescue operation was started by the remainder of the ships in the vicinity to assist the survivors of the stricken destroyer which was by now well alight.

Sea King helicopters began ferrying the injured to us, bringing them on board *Hermes* as we had the largest available sickbay. On their return flights, the helicopters took over fire-fighting gear, but it was in vain and *Sheffield* was later abandoned. Most of her uninjured survivors were plucked from her side by HMS *Arrow* (a Type 21 frigate), and all credit is due to her crew who risked their own ship close to the scorching heat of the fire raging aboard *Sheffield*. The Exocet-carrying Super Etendards had evidently known our position and had come in very low to keep below our radar horizon. They had caught us by surprise.

An aerial view of the burning HMS Sheffield.

While our minds were kept fully occupied by the tragedy of *Sheffield,* 800 Squadron suffered its own personal setback. Lieutenant Nick Taylor was shot down while on a raid over Goose Green. We later heard he was buried by the Argentinians will full military honours. It had been a tragic day but the losses seemed to strengthen everyone's resolve, particularly the doubters. Now it was clear what war was all about. The honeymoon period was over and it was now obvious that we could expect our share of pain and suffering.

For the next two weeks, until the landing ships and troops arrived in numbers, we had to play a waiting game, and this period was a curious mixture of quiet interspersed with moments of furious activity. For much of this time, the fog came in again, bringing with it the infernal 100 per cent humidity. However, breaks in the weather allowed a certain amount of flying and during these periods the Argentine spy trawler *Narwal* was successfully attacked by Sea Harriers and three Skyhawks were shot down by Sea Wolf missiles fired from *Brilliant.* During this same period, HMS *Glasgow* was hit by a bomb which fortunately sailed in one side and straight out the other without exploding.

This relatively quiet interlude was interrupted with the news of the successful commando raid on Pebble Island where a large number of Pucaras were damaged. 800 Squadron continued regularly to bomb Stanley airfield to deny its use to fast jets, and at night the frigates and destroyers continued to provide a heavy shore bombardment to keep the defenders awake and generally demoralise them.

On May 18 we were treated to an impressive sight when the main elements of the task force met up with the amphibious landing force vessels. To see so many ships was very comforting, they stretched across the whole horizon – merchant ships of every shape and colour, landing ships, escorts, and of course dwarfing them all the 'Great White Whale', the *Canberra.* It was very colourful, especially the Townsend Thoresen vessel which still sported her orange and white livery. Some ships, however, had begun camouflaging work, notably Captain Ian North's *Atlantic Conveyor.* Work was still in progress painting the superstructure grey instead of the rather striking white. She was most welcome in view of the reinforcement of Sea Harriers and RAF GR3s, plus equipment.

Over the next five days a massive re-organisation of our forces took place and the remaining troop-carrying Sea King Mk4 helicopters transferred to HMS *Fearless* or *Intrepid.* On the last ferry flight one crashed into the sea with the tragic loss of 21 lives.

The Harrier force aboard *Hermes* now grew, with the addition of four light-grey Sea Harriers of the newly formed 809 Squadron together with six RAF Harrier GR3s from No. 1 (F) Squadron, ferried over in a VTOL hop from *Atlantic Conveyor.* In addition, four other light-grey Sea Harriers from *Atlantic Conveyor* ferried to

73

A cross-section of the escorts available to the Task Force in the South Atlantic. In the centre, HMS Broadsword, *on the right a Type 21 frigate, and on the left a Type 12.*

Invincible. These extra aircraft now brought *Hermes'* total complement of jets up to 21, and we also received a few extra maintainers, including some 17 RAF personnel. These brought our squadron personnel to a modest 180, to give a ratio of less than 9 men for each aircraft. The RAF brought their own particular expertise, we provided the manpower.

Our peacetime ratio in the RN was 20 men per aircraft. A problem remained, however, in that we still had only 16 armourers, who now had to attend to an additional 10 aircraft. I think that comparison goes a long way to highlighting just how heavy our workload was and how light our manning. By now a reduced schedule wartime servicing system was in use and its successful operation became crucial with the rapidly increasing workload. As soon as the reinforcements arrived we set about checking on their damp-proofing and carried out similar work on them to that already done on the original 12. As with the RAF pilots, the RAF ground crew integrated well into the naval system. During their first two days on board, the RAF Harriers spent much of the time getting acclimatised to shipboard operations and their pilots carried out their first launches and recoveries at sea. But before continuing with the next phase of Operation Corporate, it is worth describing the sort of conditions we lived under aboard *Hermes.*

I have already explained that we were divided into two watches working in eight-hour alternating shifts. This was not a general rule in the ship, it depended which department you were in and what responsibilities you had. But the ship was operating in a war zone and everybody aboard followed strict rules and disciplines aimed at minimising losses and casualties if we were hit. Survival equipment, which consisted of a gas mask, rubber 'once only' immersion suit, lifejacket and anti-flash gear were carried at all times, even when eating, and it remained alongside when we were sleeping.

We slept in our clothes and in *Hermes,* No. 5 deck and below (below the waterline) was closed for accommodation as a precaution against torpedo attack. It was permitted to move about these decks, but certainly not to sleep there. This led to the upper decks being overcrowded as there were cabins and crew accommodation on 5 deck.

Watertight hatches and doors remained closed and clipped. Movement through the ship was slow and difficult as a result. Some of the main hatches that remained closed had what we called 'kidney' hatches set into their centres. These allow the passage of a single person through to the deck above or below, without necessitating the opening of the main hatch with all its many clips. Even so, transiting through the ship could be a slow process if you were laden down with all your gear as well. I think I discovered why they are called 'kidney' hatches – that is the exact part of the anatomy they always seem to catch when a person struggles through them!

Passage through the ship, even when remaining on one deck was not easy, not only due to the watertight rules, but also due to the large numbers of men sleeping virtually anywhere they could. For instance the wardroom became the dormitory of the lieutenants, and other areas were designated for various personnel. There were many men lying in the passageways and in machinery/equipment spaces, and yet in spite of the cold and miserably damp conditions morale remained incredibly high. Complaints were few and discipline problems non-existent. I am not sure of the precise number of personnel aboard *Hermes,* but there was certainly a good few over 2,000, which included the ship's crew, the RN and RAF squadrons of course, and the helicopter squadrons. There were also the Commandos, Special Air Service, Special Boat Service and others, including the reporters and television crews and Admiral Woodward and his staff.

At last, following this redistribution of men and materials through the task force, all was ready, and on May 21 our forces set foot once more on the Falklands, at San Carlos. The landing ships, stores-laden merchantmen and the *Canberra,* under the protection of several frigates and destroyers, had departed inshore overnight, leaving *Hermes, Invincible* and a few escorts well to the east to provide the much needed air cover.

Atlantic Conveyor *as she appeared when she joined the Task Force. Cpt North, her Master, had ordered that the ship's superstructure should be painted overall grey camouflage, an operation that was only partly completed at this stage.*

It was another hectic day and news from ashore was sparse, but in *Hermes* we were too busy providing aircraft to be concerned about that. Sea Harriers were launched on CAP at a rate of a pair every 20 minutes to provide non-stop air cover near the landing area. The operating flexibility of the Sea Harrier proved its worth time and time again, recovery to the deck in aft-facing vertical landings became commonplace and within as little time as it took to refuel and (if necessary) re-arm, the aircraft were ready to launch again.

While the Sea Harriers were flying CAPs, the GR3s were also flying in pairs in the ground attack role, dropping bombs as directed by the forces ashore. As a result of their low-level attacks, they were subjected to a higher concentration of small arms fire than the Sea Harriers and naturally the chances of being hit were increased.

That morning GR3s had suffered their first casualties when one aircraft returned with minor damage and a second became overdue. We heard later that the Harrier had been shot down but that the pilot had ejected safely, was injured and held prisoner of war.

By mid-morning on May 21 the air battle was raging fiercely as Argentine Skyhawks and Mirages came in to bomb our ships close inshore in San Carlos Water. There were waves and waves of them. It was inevitable that some of these attacks got through the cordon of defences and were pressed home. Still, to do so, the Argentine pilots had to break through the Sea Harrier CAP, into a deadly missile trap and finally into the barrage of metal thrown up by every ship and gun, from Seacat missiles to any rifle that could be brought to bear. Several warships were hit and some of them contained unexploded bombs.

Fortunately the Argentine pilots tended to go for the warships and not the landing ships. If they had the loss of life would surely have been much greater. Their aircraft losses were mounting and by nightfall 800 Squadron had claimed 5 Skyhawks and another possible, out of a total of 19 shot down that day, all against the loss of one GR3. But we later heard that HMS *Ardent* had been abandoned and that HMS *Argonaut* was badly damaged.

The next two days followed a similar pattern with nearly 50 sorties being launched from *Hermes* on May 22 alone. The GR3s' appetite for bombs was growing and the single heavy lift RAF Chinook that had been assembled and flown off *Atlantic Conveyor* was rapidly pressed into service to supply us with more ordnance from other ships in the task force. However, the enemy response was much quieter than the day before and this left time for 800 Squadron aircraft on CAP to strafe a fast patrol boat and force it ashore as well as add another Skyhawk to the tally.

As news of each success filtered back, an air of excitement spread through the ground crew and maintainers like wildfire and, on his return, the pilot would be treated to a round of backslapping and enthusiastic congratulations before being whisked below for de-

The sole surviving Chinook helicopter from Atlantic Conveyor, Bravo November.

brief by staff officers. But late in the evening of May 23 came another loss for us. During a launch for a night raid a Sea Harrier flown by Lieutenant Commander Gordon Batt appeared to fly straight into the sea shortly after take- off. Lieutenant Commander Batt was to be our last casualty but by then we were becoming hardened and had come to expect some blows. The enemy losses, however, continued to mount alarmingly and on May 24, three Mirage 5s were destroyed by one pair of aircraft, 800 Squadron's Commanding Officer, Lieutenant Commander Andy Auld, claiming two of them. On his return he was carried shoulder high from his aircraft.

Heavy enemy retaliation was expected on May 25, Argentine's National Day, and we thought this would come principally from the aircraft carrier of the same name. Initially the day went well with attacking aircraft being claimed inshore by HMS *Coventry* and *Plymouth* and the shore-based Rapier missiles. But in the evening disaster struck when *Coventry*'s defences were overwhelmed and she was hit by several bombs. She sank shortly afterwards. Our goalkeeper, HMS *Broadsword,* was with *Coventry* at the time and she escaped with a seemingly charmed life even though she took a bomb hit that went through her side and up out through her flight deck.

Lt Cdr Andy Auld is carried shoulder high on his return from shooting down two Argentine Mirages on the same sortie.

Then came our turn – or very nearly, and certainly far too close for comfort. In the past few days, all Argentine air action had been concentrated against the ships close inshore in the Falkland Sound; now the attacks came at us. Suddenly Super Etendards were detected close by, missile release was reported and their last stages of flight were supposedly observed by several people in *Hermes,* as the nearby *Atlantic Conveyor,* about three miles away at that time, was struck twice by Exocets. Within seconds the air was filled by a salvo of six Sea Dart missiles fired from HMS *Invincible,* some of which powered straight out over *Hermes* and it was believed something was hit.

As darkness fell, the flames from *Atlantic Conveyor* – alight from stem to stern – lit up the skies as yet another rescue operation was mounted. Later the stricken ship's Wessex and single Chinook helicopters found an overnight home on *Hermes* after playing their part in the search for survivors. This was the closest *Hermes* came to being hit and, once again, we found ourselves with many homeless survivors with no more possessions than the set of clothes they had been given when they arrived on board. It was a pitiful sight; all they had was toothbrush, towel, flannel and a set of number eights (day-to-day working rig).

Over the next few days, the troops ashore consolidated their positions and we continued to provide both fighter air cover and close air support. In the battle for Goose Green another GR3 was shot down and the pilot, Squadron Leader Bob Iveson, safely ejected, behind enemy lines, and evaded capture for two days before being picked up by a friendly helicopter. Our gun and missile defensive fire power was particularly successful in claiming more enemy aircraft and the current catchphrase 'as quiet as a Mirage crewroom' obviously took on stronger meaning as enemy raids were undoubtedly on the decline. By May 30, Goose Green and Douglas had been taken but our ability to launch GR3 raids in support of our ground forces was becoming very difficult, as one aircraft suffered significant shrapnel damage to its Pegasus engine during a low-level rocket attack on Stanley runway. This reduced our GR3 complement to three effectives, although on two subsequent occasions a pair of GR3s were flown non-stop, being air-to-air refuelled, from Ascension to *Hermes* to maintain No. 1 (F) Squadron at six aircraft.

The damaged aircraft was taken down into the hangar and the one-piece wing was removed for access to the engine. Unfortunately the GR3s Pegasus engine, a Mk103 is slightly different from the Sea Harrier's Mk104, so we could not install one of our own spare engines. A spare Pegasus 103 had been lost aboard *Atlantic Conveyor,* but fortunately we managed to locate another on board HMS *Intrepid.* This was airlifted over to us.

Three days of now familiar Falklands fog reduced flying to a minimum until June 5, when 800 Squadron provided the first Sea Harriers to land ashore on the temporary landing strip at San Carlos, quaintly nicknamed HMS *Sheathbill.* This was subsequently used many times and provided an invaluable refuelling facility ashore, with some pilots achieving as many as six sorties a day, flying from this 800 ft aluminium runway.

An aerial view of Atlantic Conveyor, *still burning after the Exocet hit. On her stern deck can be seen the remains of a helicopter, possibly a Chinook, and a Wessex on her main deck.*

By now we could see the end of the conflict. Setbacks were become fewer and fewer and even the loss of *Sir Galahad* and the terrible casualties suffered by the embarked Welsh Guards did nothing to reduce our optimism, as she had been hit in Bluff Cove while involved in the final build-up before the advance on Stanley. On June 8, two Sea Harriers from 800 Squadron scored a final dramatic success. A complete wave of four Mirages coming in to attack shipping inshore and straffing our ground troops, were destroyed by Flight Lieutenant Dave Morgan RAF, who hit two and Lieutenant Dave Smith RN, who shot down one. The fourth Mirage was seen to impact the sea while trying to escape.

In a last fling on June 11, their air effort expended, the Argentine defence forces fired a shore-launched Exocet which struck HMS *Glamorgan,* wiping out her flight deck and crew. The ship survived to sail home and has since been repaired and is back in service.

On June 12, the Squadron completed its thousandth sortie since leaving Portsmouth.

That night the encirclement of Stanley was complete, and at midnight on June 14 the Argentine forces on the Falklands formally surrendered. Although we felt a great sense of relief, there was no immediate celebration. With thousands of prisoners ashore and the Argentine Government unwilling to provide for their safe unmolested return, we remained at alert and continued to put up air patrols by day and maintain deck alert at night. However, Admiral Woodward must have felt confident enough as he detached HMS *Invincible* for a two-week period of self-maintenance and *Hermes* was left to hold the air defence role alone.

From the time *Hermes* entered the total exclusion zone, until the cessation of hostilities, 800 Squadron had flown over 1,000 sorties with almost as many equivalent periods spent at alert on deck with the aircraft armed and manned. Vast quantities of both aviation and ship's fuel had been used, requiring refuelling at sea every few days. This was just a small part of the colossal support effort that had been generated to meet the needs of tens of thousands of men ashore and at sea in over a hundred ships. It was a magnificent effort.

By July 2 *Invincible* had returned from her self-maintenance, during which she became the first ship to change an engine (an Olympus gas turbine) while on active duty at sea. Once again she looked neat and trim with the effects of the Falklands weather and the signs of being in action erased. We detached two of our Sea Harriers to *Invincible* that day, and on July 3 we actually anchored just off the Falklands, seeing for the first time what we had been fighting for. For many on board it was their first, and last, look at the Islands. Admiral Woodward and his staff disembarked from *Hermes* as they were to fly home in a Hercules via Ascension Island.

To emphasise the strength and the continued serviceability of

The Argentine land-launch, trailer-mounted Exocet missile unit, of the type used against HMS Glamorgan, *the last ship to be hit during the campaign.*

the *Hermes* air group prior to departure north, a massive flypast was flown from the deck over the ship and then over Stanley. It commenced with 12 helicopters and was then followed by no less than 16 Harriers – 11 RN Sea Harriers and 5 RAF GR3s. Many weeks of operations with an average of 17 Harriers on deck enabled all 16 to be launched in 5 minutes and recovered in just over 7. On July 4, the battle-scarred GR3s of No. 1 (F) Squadron disembarked to Stanley airfield and we sailed north for home.

The story of *Hermes* in the Falklands does not really end there for on the way home there were still constant reminders of what had happened. Our faithful goalkeeper, HMS *Broadsword* was still with us and when we refuelled her on the way back and she was close to, we could see her scars and the rust spots showing from her unpainted battle damage repairs. In warm sunshine – the first we had experienced for some time – we stopped only briefly at Ascension, to offload vital stores and an advance party of personnel who were required home as soon as possible, ahead of the ship. It was my task to choose about 40 names for this flight and I think on reflection that was probably one of the hardest decisions I have ever had to make. Everyone wanted to return home with the ship as one unit, to arrive back together for the homecoming that we knew would greet us.

HMS Glasgow *alongside* *HMS* Hermes *for refuelling. Just above her waterline can be seen the results of an Argentine attack.*

(left) *HMS* Illustrious *from the deck of HMS* Hermes. *The new ship completes some fast manoeuvring sequences in greeting the large carrier.*

(right) *HMS* Broadsword *increases speed to overtake HMS* Hermes *in a final salute before the two ships part company after many months of shared duties.*

Having said our farewells to the groups who disembarked to fly back ahead, we pushed on north, now safe from retaliatory attack. It was only then that we could afford to relax, and we did. The mess dinner was guaranteed to give even the hardest head a night to remember. The supply officers who had done a great job keeping us nourished, if not with interesting food, at least with filling food, were given a taste of their own medicine when they were invited to partake of some broccoli ice cream.

We finally bade farewell to *Broadsword* as we neared Gibraltar and when she accelerated past us in an impressive shower of spray, her crew opened up on us with hosepipes. They were squirting the water into the wind and none of it came anywhere near us. They on the other hand were saturated. It did not matter, but the farewell as we saw it from a packed flight deck, was something that will remain with all of us – the fast steaming frigate, the spray, the hoses and the two crews cheering each other. It was a very emotional sight.

On July 19, in the Bay of Biscay and within flying distance of the United Kingdom, 6 of the remaining 12 Sea Harriers were flown off to Yeovilton to be prepared for redeployment south again in HMS *Illustrious*. On the next day we entered the Channel and out of the morning mist we were greeted by the sight of HMS *Torquay,* her decks lined by scores of Wrens on a day trip out of Devonport. Shortly afterwards we were treated to an agile display of ship manoeuvring by *Illustrious,* her decks lined with hundreds of men cheering, clapping and waving.

Overnight we anchored in Sandown Bay to prepare for entry to Portsmouth the next day via Spithead, where we moved to at dawn. It was while we were there that the cross-Channel ferries found us and we began to get visitors shortly afterwards. Following a brief whirlwind visit by the Prime Minister, the remaining Sea Harriers were positioned for entry into harbour and the ship's crew lined the deck for 'Procedure Alpha'. By now too, we had been found by the small boat flotilla, including the inevitable young ladies unable to keep their clothes on.

A weather-beaten HMS Hermes returns to an emotional welcome at Portsmouth. Accompanying her up the harbour was a flotilla of small boats.

I cannot adequately describe our emotions as we sailed into Portsmouth. But with over a hundred small boats following us in, and thousands upon thousands of people lining the beaches and sea walls, it was probably the most moving experience any of us will ever know for the rest of our lives.

At last, on the jetty, some 10,000 of our families waited to see us in, a sea of joyful faces and banners. We were home. The next day the remaining aircraft were flown off, the Sea Kings to RN Air Squadron Culdrose and the Sea Harriers to 899 Squadron at Yeovilton. 800 Squadron, after looking after a maximum of 21 Harriers, was now temporarily reduced to zero. We went on leave.

Flight Sergeant Ray Cowburn RAF

Flight Sergeant Ray Cowburn was one of the first of the Harrier maintenance engineers from No. 1 (F) Squadron to return to RAF Wittering. He
worked in *Atlantic Conveyor,* then in HMS *Hermes* until he was transferred ashore on June 1 with a small party to Port San Carlos, where a forward operating base and re-fuelling facility had been set up by the Royal
Engineers. Sometime after recording his experiences, Flight Sergeant
Cowburn died of a heart attack in the United Kingdom and his story
appears with the permission of his widow.

I was actually in Canada on Exercise Maple Flag 9 when I was
given three hours notice to be prepared to return to the United
Kingdom. Together with others, I was picked up by an RAF
Hercules – I think it was returning from the United States – and
we were flown to an overnight stop in Newfoundland, and from
there, straight back to RAF Wittering in Northants.

A number of modifications were being embodied to the RAF
Harrier fleet immediately, the most important being the Sidewinder conversion to enable the GR3s to carry and fire AIM–9
infra-red homing missiles. In addition, we installed modifications
to I-band transponders and FINRAE, and fitted tie-down lugs to
outriggers, as the Harrier GR3s were going to operate on board
ships.

Throughout all this work we had the most amazing support
from British Aerospace, at both Kingston and Dunsfold. The
recognised number of hours in the working day were totally disre-
garded and we just carried on with the job in hand. In a very short
period we got a lot of work done.

We finally moved out on May 1, in a Hercules transport aircraft
direct to Ascension Island. The first flight of Harriers from RAF
Wittering were planned to be only a couple of days behind us, but
we had to be prepared to receive them. We stopped en route at
Gibraltar and West Africa. Two Hercules transport aircraft were
used, carrying both personnel and equipment. There were about 40
personnel from Wittering. We set ourselves up on Ascension Island
at Wideawake airfield, ready for the first arrival of the GR3s. The
first wave of two aircraft came in on May 3, followed each day by

more, until by May 5 there were nine Harriers there. The following day the aircraft embarked in *Atlantic Conveyor* by a short VTOL ferry flight.

The engineering team of 40 was split and 18 of us, made up of Flight Lieutenant Brian Mason, myself and two men from each trade, as well as one safety equipment officer and one supplier, went aboard. The others remained at Ascension as back-up, with the senior engineering officer present. This was necessary as there was a threat – albeit a faint one – of an attack on the rapidly growing military stockpiles there.

Atlantic Conveyor, with the RAF party on board, left on May 7, and as soon as we were under way we began preparing the aircraft for the journey. Unlike the Sea Harrier, the GR3 is not specially treated for operations in a maritime environment and the aircraft has a number of magnesium parts. Magnesium coming into contact with salt water sets up a reaction and corrosion sets in very quickly. We therefore had to cover the Harriers as they were exposed on *Atlantic Conveyor's* upper deck. The aircraft were not fully exposed to green water as we had a wall of containers along each deck edge and the aircraft and helicopters were protected from the worst of the weather. Nevertheless, spray could have settled on the GR3s, so we covered them with specially made anti-humidity bags. Prior to covering the aircraft with the bags, we went through an anti-corrosion protection routine. We washed the engines and then sprayed them with PX24 and sealed them. PX28 (a protective grease) was liberally applied to the undercarriage and pylons, and then we bagged up the aircraft. That was quite a challenge. We had never tried it before, but after a couple of false starts, we managed to get the technique right and after the first success the other aircraft were covered far more quickly. It certainly was hard work, though. Matters were not made any easier by the presence of the Sea Harriers of 809 Squadron and the Chinooks of 18 Squadron, which took up a lot of deck space and left us with limited working areas. Still, we got it done and that was the main thing.

We sighted the task force on about May 17, unbagged the aircraft and prepared them for cross-decking (VTOL ferrying to the carriers). Again, our engineering team was split in half, nine going on board *Hermes* to receive the aircraft, while I remained with eight others in *Atlantic Conveyor* to prepare the Harriers for the vertical launch, off the VTOL spot located forward.

Once the aircraft had been despatched from the *Atlantic Conveyor,* we had *Hermes'* helicopters lift out our 'fly-away packs', which consisted of spares, stores, avionics and parts. The final transfer of Harriers to *Hermes* was completed by May 20, the delay being caused by one unserviceable aircraft and bad weather. Because of the delay, these Harriers had to ferry across to *Invincible,* refuel and then fly on to *Hermes,* which by then was closer to the Falklands. Evidently, the carriers had taken it in turns to

A view from the bridge wing of Atlantic Conveyor *showing Sea Harrier and Harrier GR3s 'bagged up' for the journey south, protected against salt water and spray.*

approach *Atlantic Conveyor*. So, while one ship remained on watch, the other was collecting her reinforcement aircraft.

On May 21, it all happened for us. We began to feel somewhat as though we were hybrids. Here we were, RAF personnel, suddenly dropped into a naval environment. Certainly we had been in *Atlantic Conveyor*, but that was a maritime environment. This was naval. It was strange really, one doesn't think about the differences between services but there certainly are some and it took us time to acclimatise to this new enclosed fighting-ship world.

For example, in the RAF back at Wittering or wherever we went, we worked in shifts to suit the environment. No longer. The Royal Navy operates watches, and has 24 hours in its day. We divided our strength into two sections and went to work. But the two sections were not fixed as we tended to muck-in when required. Most of our rectification work was done at night. So, in effect we worked eight hours on, and eight hours off. I don't think I have ever been so tired or done so much. I was even more sorry for the naval personnel — they had been working that system since they had left home waters. And of course, even when we were off duty, we still had to respond to the alarms and the action stations bells. That was one thing, I must confess, I didn't like at all.

When we practice an alert in the RAF we go to shelters or dive into the nearest slit trench. It's your own decision as to where you go within reason when you're on a 500 acre airfield. But on board a fighting ship, you're closed up in a watertight compartment and you can't see what's happening. There were armoured bulkheads, etc., but that was not the point. We knew of the Exocet attacks later on, and we knew that, as the flagship, we would be well defended, though also a prime target.

The imagination plays tricks when you are in a strange environment and we all imagined an Exocet winging its way straight for us. Still I'll give the RN its due, the ship's command did give us a very good running commentary and that made things easier to take even when we were under threat of Exocet attack, which did happen.

The sailors were great. Initially we experienced a lot of tension between the two services, but only because they took it for granted we knew the ship's routine, what to do, where we were going, etc., while on board. Of course, we didn't. The only thing we knew on board were our GR3s. But within a short space of time we had settled down and were accepted by the RN. We helped each other because we all worked together. Sometimes you would find Fleet Air Arm (FAA) engineers giving us a hand on the GR3s and at other times we would help them with the Sea Harriers or with any other problem that happened to be around – regardless of what it was.

While at work actually preparing the aircraft for missions, we would carry out the start-up procedure and then hand over the aircraft and pilot to the RN deck crews for marshalling on the flight deck, launch and later recovery.

Surrounded as we were by hundreds of sailors, we 'light blues' became a very close-knit team – not to the point of being insular, but the clanning was quite natural. Even so we did get to know the FAA personnel quite well and very quickly, due to the situation we shared. Back at Wittering, the process would have taken much longer. And, of course, good relationships were fostered, both within our group and outside. They took a bit of a battering when an aircraft did not return. For example, when Flight Lieutenant Jeffrey Glover failed to return from his ground attack mission it hit us very hard and we all felt great concern for his safety. We didn't know at the time that he was alright, but when it was confirmed that he was alive and well, our morale rose again. Morale wasn't seriously dented by this. Our spirits were a bit down, but I would say that in the long term our morale was strengthened by the episode.

From the earlier rapid preparations to get the aircraft ready, we now increased our efforts as work demands became greater and greater. We started at about 7.00 a.m. Zulu (Greenwich mean time), as this gave us a better working day. For example, out in the Falklands, it did not get light until about 10.45 to 11.00 Zulu and we were at action stations by dawn. It got dark by 8.00 p.m. Zulu –

so it was a short daylight period. Not a short day for us though – on many occasions I started work at 7.30 a.m. and didn't finish until midnight, or once until 2.30 a.m. I still had to be up the following morning on time, though, and that went on day after day.

But the work in general went in stops and starts. One minute we were working at double speed to get the aircraft operational, and when they had gone, the waiting was a bit of an anti-climax and it was time to get some shut-eye. We would go through a frantic period again when they returned. Other times the aircraft would be on board on 5 minutes alert – and that state could remain for 2 or 3 hours at a time. The only aircraft movement during that period was the regular coming and going of RN Sea Harriers on CAP duties. Our own armourers, however, were kept busy all the time as they joined in with the FAA teams on deck.

Apart from regular servicing and rectification of minor faults, our other main task was to repair battle damage, most of which resulted from small arms fire or debris impact. The first battle damage repair we had was when a GR3 returned with hits in the starboard wing and gunpod, and the shell must have passed about a foot from the cockpit, going up from the pod and passing through at an angle to the rear. We had a joke going about that one, that if the pilot had put his hand out to signal a right turn, he would have lost it. On that same Harrier there was another hit on the starboard outboard pylon, damaging the drop tank and entering the underwing skin to dent the hydraulic power control access panel on the upper surface of the wing. Fortunately there was not too much physical destruction and it was all repaired quickly by using recommended battle damage repair methods.

An interesting modification carried out on our GR3s was the installation of a chaff dispenser. This work entailed mounting a small bracket riveted to the inside of the airbrake, to which a length of cord was attached and then connected to pre-packed chaff package wedged in the top of the airbrake bay. The idea was that when the airbrake was extended fully down, the package opened to expel its contents and provide a tin foil screen to confuse enemy radar and missiles. It worked very well. The modification was originally an RN suggestion, and later on we received proper chaff dispensers with the replacement aircraft flown in from the United Kingdom.

The aircraft stood up very well to the conditions we were operating in, and another factor that greatly assisted us was the spread of both engine and lifed component servicing times in the Harriers on board. While some were fairly new, others had just come out of major servicing, so we did not have to worry about major routine work.

Up until the time I left HMS *Hermes* to work at the temporary landing strip at Port San Carlos, we had few battle damage cases – all caused by ground fire and mainly small arms hits.

On June 1 I went ashore, flying in a helicopter from *Hermes* on to the landing ship *Sir Bedevere*. I spent the night in her as she crept up the Sound and into San Carlos Water or, as it was called, Bomb Alley. The following morning I went by landing craft out to HMS *Fearless* and was helicopter-lifted to Port San Carlos in the mid-afternoon of June 2.

It was rather a bare-looking site with many contours, and there on a slight rise was the temporary metal matting strip with two loops extending from each side at its lower end to form hardstandings for the Harriers. In fact this runway was pointing directly up the slight rise and the incline helped the pilots takeoff, rather along the same principles as the ski-jump ramps aboard the two carriers, though of course certainly not as effective.

The ground support party based there consisted of myself and one of the flight line mechanics, a chief petty officer, a petty officer and two leading seamen from the Fleet Air Arm – that was all, but it was a team effort. In effect, the metal strip at Port San Carlos became the Harriers' forward base and we remained there for about three weeks until relieved. The Argentine Air Force air attacks were regular and we spent a lot of time diving in and out of slit trenches.

On our first night ashore we scrounged a tent and were told where to pitch it. We were just settling in when a 10 ft tall (or so he seemed) sergeant major questioned the siting of our tent. And then he told us that the British troops' outer perimeter was only 15 yd

A Sea Harrier launching from the 850 ft metal runway at San Carlos.

away and there had been a report of the Argentinian equivalent of our Special Boat Service making a landing only a short way away along the coast. To add to that there was also the minor consideration of an unexploded 1,000 lb bomb nearby.

That night we stayed in the slit trenches. It was the longest 14 hours in my life, and all night along, patrols of Royal Marines were passing through, carrying out infiltrator checks.

The following day, our first full day ashore, the weather really deteriorated, and since no aircraft could land on the strip we took the opportunity of making ourselves more prepared. Once we had made ourselves more secure, we waited for the weather to lift. The strip was about 300 yd long and had been laid by the Royal Engineers. The two loops at the lower end were for refuelling – the left loop – and parking – the right. It was laid on grass and peat and this area was really the only flat piece of land in the area.

Apart from ourselves, there were detachments of troops around and we were bracketed by adjacent Rapier surface-to-air-missile batteries. Along with us, the Harrier crews, there was the sole remaining Chinook and its crew from 18 Squadron as well as Wessex and Royal Navy Sea King helicopters, all supporting the ground troops.

A series of flexible bags containing aviation fuel for the Harriers and helicopters floated on the shoreline at Port San Carlos. These had been moored inshore and connected to a pumping unit. Fuel was pumped in from the coast by pipeline. Once we started using the strip, the Harriers were able to spend more time over the islands and things got very busy for us. On one day we supported 18 to 19 Harrier and Sea Harrier movements on the small base.

The fighting continued for another two weeks after we arrived, but we had to remain on the strip for a further week before being relieved. By the end we had handled or turned round nearly 180 aircraft movements. Apart from the refuelling operations itself, we also carried out very minor repairs – I emphasise they were very minor as we had no real engineering back-up on shore. We still had our moments of excitement, however, such as the time one Harrier sank through the metal matting at one of the joints, the nosegear going in up to its landing light. We tried everything we could, but it would not move.

Eventually we called in the Royal Engineers with some heavy lift equipment and managed to get the aircraft out. Although we lifted it at the approved strengthened points, the methods we used were questionable. But we had to get that aircraft out at all costs, and out it came with no damage. It just goes to show how robust the aircraft is.

Following that episode, the Royal Engineers team filled in the holes and strengthened the support underneath. This de-bogged Harrier then started up, and off it went, none the worse for its experience.

We had another similar Harrier incident, but this time the nose

A close-up view of the sole surviving Chinook helicopter, Bravo November, as it closes with HMS Hermes.

wheel ran off the metal matting and sank down. But we had very little trouble lifting that one out. We were expecting more problems like that, as the strip was only half as wide again as the Harrier's wheel tracks, but all went smoothly.

While most aviation facilities in the area were somewhat crude, we boasted a flight line office. It belonged to the settlement at Port San Carlos and was made of corrugated iron. It measured about 6 × 5 × 6 ft. That was spacious.

While we were at the strip, one of the Harriers, flown by Wing Commander Peter Squire of No. 1 (F) Squadron, had a problem

Stanley Airfield after the cessation of hostilities. In the foreground can be seen the water-filled crater made by a 1000 lb bomb dropped by a Vulcan bomber. This was the nearest bomb burst to the runway.

whilst landing. In fact, he could have ejected, but he decided to stay with the aircraft, and experienced a somewhat heavy landing on the grass near the strip. It careered right across the metal strip, severing it, and continued its course up the hill and over the brow finally stopping straddled across a slit trench normally reserved for a Rapier battery's crew. The Royal Engineers soon repaired the runway by taking up some of the matting from further back and replacing the damaged area, and at the same time we got rid of one of the taxi loops as the ground was proving unsuitable.

On June 22 we left the metal strip and went on board the *St Edmund* joining the main party of No. 1 (F) Squadron, which had

(top) A wrecked Pucara at Port Stanley.

(bottom) Argentine Aermacchi 339 with ejection seats blown.

sailed south after we had left – the others of our RAF party were still in *Hermes*. We were taken to Port Stanley airfield, where we spent a couple of days carrying out a reconnaissance of the area looking for a suitable operating base there. While we were looking around the area, we still slept on board *St Edmund*, but on June 26 we moved to Stanley airfield itself to set up our quarters.

What a mess it was! The state of the airfield was appalling, as it had been used as a prisoner-of-war camp after the ceasefire. Wherever you looked there was abandoned equipment, clothes, helmets, bayonets – and filth. The airfield itself was quite badly damaged with big craters caused by the 1,000 lb bombs and smaller ones from the cluster bombs. There were a lot of unexploded bombs and cluster bomblets lying around. In addition, there was a wide variety of live ammunition, ranging from 7.62 mm to 9 mm to mortar bombs and howitzer shells – I think the latter were 105 mm. There were acres of such nasty relics.

Mixed in with all that there were quite a few damaged aircraft – Pucaras and other propeller-driven jobs. The ejection seats in the Pucaras had been set off to safeguard against inadvertent firing by sightseers and souvenir collectors. There was also a strong possibility of booby traps. The aircraft looked brand new – they did not have those slicks of grease and oil one expects to see on aircraft that have seen some service.

In fact, a lot of the Argentine equipment looked new. The radar units around the airfield, Volkswagen machinery, and a lot of new-looking US and European equipment. In addition there was also a lot of 'war surplus gear' – old US-style helmets and webbing, etc. – all discarded and lying around in untidy heaps, thrown down by thousands of prisoners. One thing very noticeable was the amount of cold-weather clothing around. Piles of it.

The RAF's Harriers finally joined us ashore on July 4 – most appropriately US Independence Day – and I began my journey home on July 5.

Sergeant David Frost RAF

Aged 31, joined RAF in 1968 and is married.

When Flight Sergeant Cowburn was detached ashore to establish the ground facilities and forward base at Port San Carlos, I remained on board *Hermes* with the majority of the RAF engineering team. Our task continued as before, routine servicing and turnround operations on the GR3s, mixed in with battle damage repairs.

One aircraft returning from a sortie was particularly spectacular. A single bullet had hit the GR3 aft on the starboard side, passing rearwards and upwards through the rear reaction control system ducting in the rear equipment bay. When the pilot decelerated for vertical landing with the nozzles down, the RCS was pressurised by high-pressure – and high-temperature – bleed air, and the rear of the aircraft started smoking. The pilot was advised to come in to land immediately, about midway along the deck, which was the clearest area at that time. The rear RCS duct, as it was damaged, was leaking quantities of very hot air. By the time the aircraft recovered on deck, the rear fuselage was cooking nicely and a lot of paint had been burnt off or was smouldering, in certain areas right down to the bare metal.

As soon as he had touched down and shut the fuel cock, the pilot got out rather quickly. We smothered the entire tail section with carbon dioxide. Even though the aircraft skin was cooling, it was still too hot to go near, let alone touch. In total that aircraft was out of service for only about 36 hours and suffered no permanent damage.

Another pilot was also very lucky. When he landed we discovered a 20 mm shell had hit the port side of the cockpit, just forward of his legs missing them by only a matter of inches. The shell hit a clamp in the air-conditioning system, shattering it and smashing it out through the starboard side, leaving a larger hole, and passing through the weapon control panel wiring loom. The shell remained in the aircraft and was recovered later, when the GR3 landed and we had a look at the damage. It seemed rather messy and complicated to repair, but as it turned out it was relatively straightforward. We cut a large hole in the skin on the portside around the shell's entry point, then pulled the wiring out through the hole and repaired the wiring outside the aircraft. That made it much easier and quicker.

A repaired drop tank.

The electricians found that normal repair techniques would have made the loom a restrictive diameter, so they painstakingly soldered each of the damaged wires and then fitted a rubber sleeve over the repaired area – it worked well. The exit hole on the starboard side was also easy to repair and was a straightforward insert patch repair job. We all found that the Harrier became with practice easy to repair, especially skin panels. Considering the damage some of the aircraft received, they were out of action for a surprisingly short time.

As with the re-arming and refuelling teams, we had naval assistance with repairs and vice versa. The RN's hangar teams were also very heavily involved with battle damage repair. This was as varied as one might expect under those conditions. We would find ourselves repairing skin panels, wiring, ducts, wind screens, canopies, drop tanks – virtually every element of the Harrier.

We had one repair which I think was the first ever such job of its kind. One aircraft returned with a hole in one of its 100 gallon drop tanks, which are made of glass fibre. Eventually we found a way to repair it. We drilled out the hole, getting rid of the rough edges, and then used two penny washers embedded in silicone-rubber tank sealant with a bolt through the middle pulling them together. It worked. Other than that we were also patching drop tanks by riveting plates on to the outside.

One Harrier needed an engine change. We were not carrying spare Pegasus engines on board the flagship and only two had been shipped out with us. Unfortunately, one of them was deep in the hull of the *Atlantic Conveyor,* now under water. However, the other had been loaded at Ascension Island on to HMS *Intrepid,* so it was comparatively nearby and accessible.

The only GR3 engine change. Carried out by a small combined team of RAF and RN personnel, the engine change was completed over three days in intermittent bursts, when other operationally necessary work permitted.

Of course the engine change did take us longer than at RAF Wittering. We disconnected the systems and prepared the engine for lifting. When it came to the actual lift, the RN preferred to do it themselves as we had never used, or even seen, the on-board equipment. The *in situ* Pegasus came out alright, but when it came to putting the new one in there were alignment problems. As we in the RAF had greater experience in engine changes than the RN ratings, we stepped in to help. That sort of action was typical of the work on board – everyone got down to it together regardless of which service they belonged to. The working relationships were particularly good.

That engine change took nearly 60 hours, but that was to be expected as we were at sea, a small team, and still working on the serviceable aircraft returning from missions as well. So, in and among the regular and more urgent work, we helped with the engine change when we had some relatively spare time.

We had 5 Harrier GR3s operational most of the time. Sometimes this might drop to 4 or (rarely) 3, but the fleet was back to 5, sometimes 6, by the following day. On average one Harrier GR3 was out of action at any one time due to servicing or battle damage repair. On the whole I would say that we did better than expectations and the achieved sortie total against loss rate was much higher than the experts had predicted.

All six of the RAF Harriers in *Hermes* had left the ship by July 5 to deploy to Port Stanley itself. Not that the RN wanted to get rid of us, but things were still cramped on board, and it was good to return to land, even though it was blowing gales and snowing by the time we arrived ashore.

I left the Falklands with Flight Sergeant Cowburn and returned via Ascension Island to a rousing welcome at RAF Wittering.

Lieutenant Commander Tony Ogilvy AFC, RN

Lieutenant Commander Anthony Ogilvy, AFC, RN (36), was the first Royal Navy Sea Harrier pilot to return to the United Kingdom from the Falklands. Married, with three sons, Lieutenant Ogilvy contracted an ear infection during the crisis, which prevented him from continuing flying. He remained in his ship, however, (HMS *Hermes,* flagship of the task force) and was able to contribute to the planning and programming of both air defence and attack operations in liaison with ship and staff officers. He was on board HMS *Hermes* when the air battle reached its peak in late May 1982 and returned to the United Kingdom in June, in a group which included all survivors from *Atlantic Conveyor*. His account follows.

At the time Argentinian forces were invading the Falklands, I was assigned to 899 Headquarters and Training Squadron at Royal Naval Air Station Yeovilton, having just commenced a refresher course on the Sea Harrier, in preparation for taking over command of 801 Squadron from Lieutenant Commander Nigel Ward. Once the decision was taken to send the task force, all three Sea Harrier Squadrons at Yeovilton put a rapid mobilisation plan into operation, prior to embarking in their ships at the beginning of April 1982. This plan even included recalling pilots on exchange tours from Australia and the United States.

801 Squadron joined HMS *Invincible,* 800 Squadron went to HMS *Hermes* and 899 Squadron was split between the two ships to augment the two frontline squadrons. I embarked in HMS *Hermes,* alongside in Portsmouth, and we sailed south on April 5 when all storing had been completed. The passage to Ascension Island was spent in working up both the air group and ship's company, with regular action and emergency station drills in preparation for the forthcoming operation.

One of the earliest changes was to repaint the Sea Harriers in a colour scheme more appropriate to the South Atlantic. The original top side colour of dark sea grey was retained and the underside painted the same shade. Wartime roundels, i.e. without the white circle, and a small aircraft serial number, were retained for identification purposes. The new colour scheme was *most* effective at low level over land or water – the aircraft virtually disappeared.

Armed with Sidewinder air-to-air missiles and 30 mm guns, Sea Harriers parked on the flight deck.

At Ascension Island we had our first taste of things to come – a sonar contact, and the fleet went to action stations for real. From then on *Hermes* remained in a high state of readiness and watertight integrity, and drills were practised with increasing regularity as we headed south.

From the start the primary role of both carriers was fleet air defence. But *Hermes* with her large and varied magazine – 1,000 lb bombs, cluster bombs, etc. – was also tasked with a number of attack options. These were against ship and land targets and, as the Squadron air warfare instructor, I was involved in a fair amount of planning en route to the total exclusion zone. Combat air patrols were carried out on an escalating scale, with increasing numbers of missions each day as the task force came closer to the Falklands. It was a Sea Harrier from 801 Squadron in HMS *Invincible* that made the first interception of the Argentine Air Force Boeing 707 reconnaissance aircraft on April 25. No aggressive action was taken in this first encounter as the rules of engagement were still very limiting.

CAPs were being flown at between 60 and 80 miles from the task force and, during the approach to the total exclusion zone, a good deal of night flying was taking place. We had no accurate knowledge of what we would be facing inside the zone and were preparing for everything. So, until we could quantify the threat, our exercises covered a wide range of tactical possibilities: new attack

97

modes like loft delivery were tried for the first time and live weapons were dropped to check arming and release circuits.

In late April and early May, well south of Ascension Island, plans for the air attack on Port Stanley airfield were being finalised. I was responsible for working out the attack profile and, with a team to assist, produced the basic plan.

In view of the intelligence reports of anti-aircraft artillery defences on and around the airfield, I decided on two complementary attack profiles using a total of nine aircraft. Four Sea Harriers would go in first to neutralise the AAA, closely followed by the remaining five which would concentrate on dropping ordnance on to Stanley airfield. It needed really accurate timing to be effective and to minimise the risk of attrition.

Using the aircraft's self-contained navigation, heading and attitude reference system (NAVHARS), the formation of nine Sea Harriers flew direct to a waypoint north-west of the island and from there the first four, led by myself, dog-legged over the sea to run in for the fire suppression attack. The other five Sea Harriers, led by the commanding officer, flew a co-ordinated navigational leg before turning in for their attack run approaching over the land.

This was the first time ever we had operationally used the loft or toss bombing technique in the Sea Harrier. It involves an approach at 100 feet flying about 520 knots to a pull-up point 3 miles or so short of the target, from where the bombs are lobbed, like in an underarm cricket-ball delivery.

The initial formation carried variously fused 1,000 lb high-explosive bombs designed to destroy AAA and radar defences and hamper repair work. Once the ordnance had been released, we went through the normal escape manoeuvre and cleared out. The loft-bombing system proved very successful, and those in the second wave on their run-in could see the airburst weapons exploding in the planned area. On pull-up, my radar warning receiver gave a locked radar alarm which reinforced our suspicions that there was an anti-aircraft missile system on the airfield. I completed a sharp escape manoeuvre and the warning cleared.

The other five Sea Harriers in the meantime attacked from the north and the north-west, aiming to produce maximum disruption to both surface and support areas. Four of the Sea Harriers were carrying cluster bombs while the fifth was armed with three 1,000 lb high-explosive bombs. They flew in at very low level, jinking hard until just before weapon release.

Apart from the runway itself, the pilots in the second wave were briefed to attack anything of value, which included hangars and buildings, oil and fuel dumps as well as parked aircraft – of which there were quite a few, including some Pucaras.

An RAF Vulcan had attacked the airfield only a few hours before us and that meant the defences were on top line. As it was, only one Harrier was hit (in the tail) and this turned out to be minor damage, repairable in a short time once back on board. The attack was a success, all the bombs were released on target and caused a considerable amount of damage.

Later that day the first Argentine air attacks were mounted, using Mirage IIIs. Two of them were detected approaching at high level and two Sea Harriers were launched from HMS *Hermes* to intercept. As they closed the targets, one Mirage fired an air-to-air guided missile which failed to hit, the targeted Sea Harrier evading the missile's flight path. The second Sea Harrier locked on to one Mirage and fired a Sidewinder at long range. It hit and the Mirage exploded. Meanwhile the second Mirage turned tail at long range and was not engaged.

Following the first interception using Sea Harriers, we continued our programme of land attacks and photo-reconnaissance over the Falklands – Pebble Island, Fox Bay, Port Stanley, Goose Green, etc. The Admiral and his staff needed as much tactical information and detailed reconnaissance data as possible and I think he was pleased by the results of these recce sorties. Certainly subsequent land operations proved the value of this work, which in later weeks was shared with the RAF Harriers of No. 1 Squadron.

While continuing our operations over Argentinian strongpoints we had our first casualty, Lieutenant Nick Taylor RN, whilst attacking installations at Goose Green. The sortie itself was successful, but of course it was tinged with great sorrow. In the back of our minds we had all expected this might happen but it came as a jolt all the same. I think it was much worse for the families at home. They would hear news reports of a Harrier pilot being shot down or involved in an accident, and all they could do was to sit and wait.

It was confirmed that there was a continuing requirement to bomb installations at Port Stanley airfield, for which both carriers devised medium-level bombing techniques. These attacks kept the airfield defenders on permanent alert as well as achieving an unquantifiable amount of damage. The raids continued on a daily basis and later attacks were made, using the loft mode by day and night aimed at the runway itself.

Later in May, additional Sea Harriers of 809 Squadron and some RAF Harrier GR3s of No. 1 (F) Squadron arrived via *Atlantic Conveyor* and were split between the two carriers, making a grand total at one stage of 22 Harriers on board HMS *Hermes*. Those plus the resident helicopter and fixed-wing squadrons made for very full carriers.

The RAF Harriers did a fine job in ground attack and reconnaissance missions, and their arrival released more Sea Harriers for air defence duties, which were becoming increasingly heavy. The San Carlos landing marked the beginning of the main air attacks by the Argentine Air Force.

The Sea Harriers in both carriers were now committed to CAP duties, and operations were stepped up to provide patrols in support of the San Carlos beach-head. After leaving their respective carriers, the Sea Harriers usually came under the tactical control of the screening ships, usually Type 42 destroyers, occasionally Type 22 frigates, but much of the intercept work was autonomous, with the Sea Harriers on CAP picking up the raids as they came in at low level.

The air defence ships in the San Carlos area did a marvellous job and HMS *Brilliant* in particular deserves a special mention. Whilst under heavy attack herself, the first lieutenant, using the ship's radar, directed Sea Harrier patrols on to raids approaching to attack at very low level. Anything I can say would never do justice to the bravery and dedication shown by those ships and their crews in the Sound.

Every day, throughout the Argentine raids, we were running a programme in *Hermes* that often required up to ten Sea Harriers at any one time. All this, with aircraft on alert throughout the night, was a tremendous task for the pilots involved, particularly the night team. They, at the height of the air battle would spend up to 10 hours in 24 in the cockpit, either flying or at alert.

By now the great strength of the Sea Harrier was becoming apparent. Under operational conditions, the aircraft and systems held up beyond anyone's expectations. Of the 16 or so Sea Harriers on board, at least 10 were serviceable at any one time. The Pegasus engine, also, more than proved its worth. During the time that I was embarked, not one Sea Harrier needed an engine change. But I think, most important of all, the aircraft *worked* so well in all roles. Every Sidewinder missile launched correctly; not once did the Aden guns fail; and all bombs separated properly fused and they all functioned. The avionics held up well, with few spares needed, and even with a very occasional degraded weapon aiming system, missiles and bombs still hit their targets. The F95 reconnaissance camera did not let us down and the aircraft showed that it can take battle damage.

As for its primary role as a fighter, the 23+ Argentine aircraft shot down – mostly Mirages and A4s – with no Sea Harrier lost in air combat says it all. The Falklands crisis has demonstrated the full extent of the Sea Harrier's capability in all its roles. It is a tough and reliable combat aircraft and, teamed with the Sidewinder AIM–9L, won the air battle hands down. It is surely no exaggeration to say that without the Sea Harrier there could have been no task force.

At one period in the deployment, HMS *Hermes* was flying 40 Harrier sorties a day, at times in appalling weather – less than 200 feet cloud base and well under half a mile visibility, in sea states that only the South Atlantic can provide. Harrier recoveries (the decelerating transition to a hover with subsequent vertical landing) came in to the deck from all angles: over the bows, up the wake and over the stern, from port or from starboard: with touchdowns amidships, on the afterdeck and just behind the bow ski-jump. Because of the ever-constant threat of hostile submarines, the Admiral preferred to steam the task force at 15 knots or so, and it

Minus one Sidewinder (which scored a 'kill'), a Sea Harrier of 800 Squadron returns victorious to HMS Hermes.

would have been tactically very unsound to turn the carrier into the wind for every launch and recovery as would have been necessary with a flat-top operating conventional naval jets.

Taking a general overall view of the Falklands operation as far as the Sea Harriers were concerned, we in the Fleet Air Arm were more than satisfied with its achievements and with the operational results. The new fixed wing RN squadrons more than justified their existence; surely now there can be no doubt anywhere of what the Sea Harrier is capable of accomplishing. Once again, as so often in the past, the RN has pioneered new techniques in naval aviation and proved them to a watching world.

Lieutenant David Smith RN

Lieutenant David Smith (27), single, joined the Royal Navy from school, entering Dartmouth in 1973. He spent five years as a ship's navigator, then went on to flying training in October 1978. He started on the Bulldog and progressed through the Jet Provost before being posted to RAF Valley for advanced flying training and RAF Brawdy for tactical weapons and air-to-air combat training. He joined 800 Squadron in February 1982.

On the day the carriers sailed I was 'goofing' illegally, on No. 2 deck in HMS *Hermes* and watching the departure. It was amazing, I have never seen anything like it. The shores were quite black with thousands of people, it was an unbelievable send-off.

Initially I was among the lucky ones. I had my own cabin and remained in comparative luxury until the Admiral came aboard at Ascension, when I was relegated to the Wardroom floor along with dozens of others. I do not think I have ever seen a ship so crowded, there were sailors, officers, Royal Marines, etc., everywhere, in every imaginable nook and cranny. Some sleeping, some cleaning rifles and equipment and others doing their 'keep fit' exercises. One of the best things about being a pilot was that one was able to get away from it all from time to time, albeit for a comparatively short period. Not that I was complaining, I was enjoying being back at sea again.

Prior to our arrival in the total exclusion zone and the first bombing attack on Port Stanley, my activities were much the same as those of any other member of the squadron. I did not take part in the first raid but spent most of my time on CAP on one or other of the three patrol zones to the west, north-west and south-west of the islands.

In the early stages of the campaign, once we had arrived at the Falklands, while some aircraft would be on CAP, others would be on alert 5 on deck. Alert 5 could be very tedious. We would sit for hours in the cockpit ready to go with nothing happening. And then suddenly there would be a scramble and the adrenalin would start pumping madly. The launch followed and then an hour of terror as we flew out to do battle with the Argentine Air Force. When we located the enemy, sometimes he got the first shot in and it was only by relying on him missing that we could close for combat. Fortunately the Argentine Air Force was fairly stretched as they

*A Sea Harrier of 809 Squad-
ron aboard HMS* Hermes
prepares to launch for CAP.

were operating some way from their bases and did not have the fuel
to mix it in the combat zone for very long. There is no doubt in my
mind that the waiting was the worst part, it was as tiring and
effort-consuming as flying.

A typical day for me would begin an hour before lunchtime – it
only got light at 1100 hours local time and was dark at 1730 hours
– when we would muster in the ship's Number 1 briefing room to
receive important information such as the ship's position, course
and speed and the various call signs. In addition, it was also vital to
know the locations or whereabouts of other escort vessels as we had
to avoid their air defence firing zones when we returned to the
carrier.

After signing out, we had our aircraft allocated and we would
then go on to the flight deck to carry out our external checks of the
aircraft. It always seemed absolute bedlam on the flight deck.
Apart from the normal 30 knots of wind over the deck, there were
helicopters landing and taking off, people shouting unintelligible
orders at God knows who and aircraft being shuffled from one side
of the deck to the other and back again for no apparent reason.

Finally, with only four minutes to go for launch, I would get into
the cockpit and carry out the internal checks. It is always at this
point that the harness snags on something or the umbilical cord to
the 'G' suit gets in the way and has to be untangled. It is moments
like these that can be the greatest danger to a pilot. The cockpit
checks are important – a pilot's life depends on them – and they
must be done properly. So in spite of being hassled and with the
straps and cord getting in the way, the pilot still has to force him-

self to go through the procedures, even though he can see 'Wings'
looking at his watch and you know he is muttering, 'Why hasn't
R4 started up yet?'

Finally, with the clock still ticking away, the checks are complete. Here we go – fuel boost pumps on, start selected, master
pressed, GTS winding up, HP fuel cock on – here we go – jet pipe
temperature rising – she's turning and burning. The navigation
system takes two minutes to align so, without further ado, I in-
itiate that process and sit it out. One-and-a-half minutes to go and
it looks as though we might just make it.

The aircraft deck handlers are now unlashing my aircraft. I
check that the ejection seat safety pins are out – otherwise I would
not be able to get out should the need arise – and I have now completed all my pre-take-off checks and the navigation system is on
line – all with 15 seconds to go to launch time.

The Flight Deck Officer (FDO) gives me the wind-up signal
slam the engine throttle to half-power to check that acceleration
time is within the permitted 3 to 4.5 seconds. The nozzles checked, I
accept the launch by showing the flat of my hand on the canopy.
The FDO's hand drops and I smash the throttle forward. Ten tons
of Pegasus thrust arrive in the small of my back in just under two
seconds and the Sea Harrier roars down the deck. A quick glance at
the RPM and temperature – looking good – and in less than three
seconds my air speed is around 90 knots and here comes the ramp.
We're off. As soon as I'm clear of the ramp I rotate the nozzles to 35
degrees down and hold everything, trying to resist the temptation
to touch the controls. She reaches the end of the trajectory and I
gently ease the nozzles forward, landing gear and flaps up, and the
aircraft is now accelerating through the 400 knot mark before I can
draw breath.

A quick radio call to the FDO – I'm holding her down to 200 ft
until I've got 500 knots and now pulling back on the stick and
pointing the nose at the top of an enormous cloud above me. She
passes through 15,000 ft effortlessly and I roll over on my back to
bring my rate of ascent under control. The FDO has given me a
vector and off we go looking for the enemy aircraft.

The sheer distance we had to transit to the combat zone limited
the amount of time we could spend on task. We always flew as pairs
so that we could give each other support and cross-cover. It also enabled us to put four missiles into a target as opposed to two with a
singleton aircraft. Once in the combat zone the patrol was always
flown in an atmosphere of crackling tension. I discovered muscles
in my neck I never knew existed, from the constant searching of
every inch of the sky for the enemy.

We could spend about 20 minutes as a rule in the zone before we
had to return, and that was usually preciously short of fuel. The recovery to the ship is always just as demanding and after an
arduous patrol it can be quite testing.

At two-and-a-half minutes to my 'Charlie' (land-on) time, I 'slot',

Ski-jump launch to CAP.
Note the weapons on deck:
Sidewinders, 1000 lb bombs
and aerial torpedoes.

which involves flying up the starboard side past the ship's bridge at 600 ft and breaking down wind for the recovery. It is from now on that the pilot of a Harrier really has to switch on and keep his act together. The flight profile has to change from being fully wingborne to fully jetborne in a hover while at the same time flying a tight fuel critical circuit to land on a small sometimes highly mobile deck.

So with my speed decaying through 300 knots, I bank down full flap, steadying the jet downwind at 600 ft. Speed below 250 knots – landing gear going down and 40 degrees of nozzle selected. Turning finals now, checking four 'greens' to indicate landing gear down and locked, hydraulics OK and duct pressure reading to my reaction controls. Halfway round the turn and descending, glide path looking good, angle of attack pegged at eight units and power coming on as I take 60 degrees nozzle. Speed dropping through 200 knots, water injection coming on and rolling out wings level for the final approach.

Nozzles to the hover stop. The speed now reducing very rapidly and power being fed on to replace wing lift. I pay very careful attention to the angle of attack and the side slip indicator, as this is the most dangerous phase of flight in the Harrier. Coming up alongside the ship and I stabilise in the hover. I glance in-board to check the engine and fuel. The latter gauge is rushing down now at

A Sea Harrier about to commence rearward taxiing in reverse thrust on the flight deck of HMS Hermes.

about 200 lb a minute as I hold nearly full power in the hover. Once steady, I move sideways crossing the deck edge, and once over my landing spot I descend quickly, bang on the deck, throttle slammed closed and nozzles fully back – taxi into a clear area where the aircraft is once again lashed down and I shut down the engine.

To go back to the combat aspects, we often had moments of bitter frustration when we would arrive over the Falklands just as an Argentine raid was leaving, or we would have to leave due to our fuel state just as one was building up. In addition, because of the distance to the three CAP zones and the number of aircraft we had, it was not always possible to cover all three areas all the time, and inevitably there were gaps in the aerial coverage and the Argentines got through. Having said that, it should be emphasised that the majority did not get through the defence rings of fighters, missiles and guns.

It was on May 24 that my fighting war really began and I fired in anger for the first time. I was flying number two to the Boss, Lieutenant Commander Andy Auld, Commanding Officer of 800 Naval Air Squadron, on CAP to the north of Pebble Island. We had just arrived in the zone when we received an 'area warning red' call from HMS *Broadsword* which was on radar picket duty. Using her pulse doppler radar, she had picked up incoming aircraft and we were called in to intercept.

We were flying up at 10,000 ft at the time and were vectored to 260 degrees diving down to the surface at high speed. I slammed the throttle and tucked myself in behind the Boss, about 100 yards away. As we passed through 550 knots, we were down to about 150 ft and began a hard turn towards the rapidly approaching enemy. Suddenly the Boss called 'visual' and there they were – four Mirages coming in very low and very fast.

As I picked them up, the Boss rolled in behind and fired both his Sidewinders in quick succession – both hit and two Mirages exploded in violent fireballs. The second pair broke hard right and I locked on to one of them. As I did so I saw him bang off his tanks and bombs to improve his manoeuvrability. As my missile 'cross' flashed across his tail, I heard the acquisition growl of the Sidewinder in my headset. I pressed the lock button, released the safety catch and fired. Fractions of a second later there was a flash from under my wing as the Sidewinder leapt off its pylon rails.

At first I thought I had missed, as the Sidewinder shot off to the right and was not heading towards the Mirage. What was not immediately apparent though was that the Sidewinder had already worked out the interception angle and was off cutting the corner to reach the Mirage. Sure enough, as the Mirage was moving across my front from left to right, the Sidewinder zeroed in on his hot tail pipe and impacted him.

There was another flash and a fireball with the Mirage breaking up and impacting the ground in a burning inferno. It was an incredible sight. In less than five seconds we had destroyed three enemy aircraft. Now for the fourth, but where was he? Suddenly I saw him under the Boss, heading west at high speed. As I still had one Sidewinder left, we turned hard and followed him. We were both going flat out for some minutes, with me just out of missile range. But we were by then getting low on fuel so we had to break off, but we heard later that he too had run out of fuel and had to ditch on his return home.

On my return, I had regained my composure enough to begin to analyse how I felt. Naturally I was pleased at having been able to help prevent a raid getting through to our ground forces, but at the same time I remember feeling horrified at seeing my first kill and saddened at having to witness and then be instrumental in the death of fellow pilots, albeit enemies at that time. No one really wins in a war. I recall reading a quote by the Duke of Wellington who after the battle of Waterloo said something like: 'The one thing more tragic than defeat is victory.'

My next eventful CAP was on June 8, the day *Sir Galahad* was hit. I was patrolling at 10,000 ft with Flight Lieutenant Dave Morgan and we could see the awful sight of the ships burning at Bluff Cove. The smoke was pouring out, thick and oily, and the entire after section of the ship was glowing red with the heat. It was about 1800 hours and getting dark when we noticed some Mirages having a go at some landing craft coming down from the direction of Goose Green. Dave rolled upside down and pulled hard for the surface.

I followed him down fast, but he was nearly disappearing in the gloom. It was very hard to keep an eye on him. I slammed the throttle to full power and aimed in the general direction in which Dave had by now disappeared. He must have been about half a mile ahead of me. My air speed was just over 600 knots when I saw

DAVID SMITH

HMS Illustrious *manoeuvring around the homeward-bound HMS* Hermes.

two bright flashes from the direction of Dave's aircraft – he had fired both Sidewinders. I watched the white smoke trails and they ended in two fireballs as the Mirages disintegrated and hit the sea.

Now where had he got to? Fortunately he opened up on the other two Mirages with his cannon and I just flew towards the shell splashes in the water – there he was. As I approached for an attack, Dave was in the way, but fortunately pulled out and cleared from my sights. I pointed the missile at the nearest bogey and heard the growl in my ears as the missile acquired him. I fired, thinking he was too far and going too fast for the missile to get him. The range was two or two-and-a-half miles, and as I watched the Sidewinder's trail it seemed to me that it flamed out about 300 yards short of its target. Evidently it did not, as there was a blinding flash, followed fractions of a second later by the Mirage impacting the ground.

We could not stay around any longer as, again, our fuel states were getting low and we had to turn for home. We sent up to high level for the long flight back to the carrier and the recovery at the end of that was not particularly easy, being one of our first night landings.

With the Argentine surrender, we carried on with CAP as we were still not sure of the state of play. Even when the carrier set off for her return journey to the United Kingdom, we still mounted CAP sorties until Ascension Island, just to be on the safe side. Even there I was scrambled to intercept two Russian Bear reconnaissance aircraft that were snooping around the area.

I was one of the pilots to fly off *Hermes* while we were still in the Bay of Biscay to return aircraft urgently needed at Yeovilton, where they were to be prepared to be sent back down south again, this time in HMS *Illustrious*. On July 20 I was flown back on board *Hermes* by helicopter for the return to Portsmouth on the following day. Four weeks later I embarked HMS *Illustrious* with 809 Sea Harrier Squadron for the return to the Falklands. There we acted as guardship until October, when the defences were able to stand on their own with the RAF Phantoms in the air defence role and Rapier surface-to-air-missile batteries fully emplaced.

108

Plate 3

An unusual view of HMS Broadsword *and the fleet tanker*
Tidespring *from the island of HMS* Hermes.

Two Sea Harriers return to HMS Hermes *at dusk after completing their*
combat air patrol over the Falklands.

Plate 4

Armed with 1,000 lb bombs, three RAF GR3s of No 1 (F) Squadron line up on the Ski-jump runway of HMS Hermes ready for launch on a dawn sortie.

A Sea Harrier launches from HMS Hermes. The very high atmospheric humidity encountered in the southern ocean winter can be appreciated from the condensation on the deck and the aircraft.

Plate 5

The fleet tanker Tidespring *refuelling HMS* Hermes *underway.*

Removing the wing of a GR3 in the hangar of HMS Hermes, *prior to engine change. Both RN and RAF maintenance crews combined their expertise during this operation.*

Plate 6

HMS Exeter *crosses the bow of HMS* Hermes

HMS Hermes *at anchor in Sandown Bay off the Isle of Wight before her triumphant entry to Portsmouth and the unforgettable welcome home.*

The Harrier Family: 25 years of V/STOL

'If a man will begin with certainties he shall end in doubts; but if he will be content with doubts, then he shall end in certainties'
(Francis Bacon, 1561–1626).

In 1956 a French engineer by the name of Michel Wibault approached Bristol Aero Engines (now Rolls-Royce Ltd, Bristol), through the US-sponsored Mutual Weapon Development Agency in Paris, with a proposal for a Gyropter, a short take-off and landing aircraft in which the thrust could be moved through an arc, or vectored, from horizontally rearward to vertically downward. The power unit was to be an 8000 hp Bristol Orion turboprop driving four centrifugal blowers, the casings of which could be rotated to direct their jets of compressed air – and therefore the thrust – through an arc of 90 degrees.

Bristol Aero Engines were not much impressed by the practicality of Wibault's original design. It was mechanically complex and too heavy to allow a useful aircraft to be proposed. The concept of vectoring the thrust, however, was exciting. It had many advantages over previous powerplant designs for an aircraft intended for V/STOL.

Design studies continued at Bristol, however, and a much more practical powerplant design was evolved and given the number BE53/1. It combined an Orpheus compressor with the first three fan stages of the Olympus, and was a major step in the right direction. But only part of the engine's thrust was vectorable and it would not have been satisfactory for military aircraft. It was at this stage that proposal brochures came to the attention of the Hawker design team at Kingston.

Innovative interchange between the design teams in Bristol and Kingston rapidly resulted in the BE53 taking a configuration which promised to provide a really practical solution, making use of four rotable nozzles. Since those early BE53 engine designs in 1957, almost every component has been changed, but the thermodynamic and mechanical arrangement of the engine has remained unaltered. Only a year after Michel Wibault brought his idea to the United Kingdom, the design team at Kingston produced the first drawings of the new aircraft – recognisably a Harrier. But at that time, the name Harrier was a long way off and the design, as was the custom at Kingston, was referred to as P (for Project) 1127 (the next serial in the project office register). The label P1127 was to become one of the most memorable of the Hawker series, which started in 1939 with the P1001 – the four-cannon Hurricane.

The P1127 was further refined during 1957–8 by the Kingston design team led by the late Sir Sydney Camm, working closely with Dr (now Sir) Stanley Hooker's team at Bristol. In its early stages the venture was entirely company-supported, though by 1958 the engine was 75 per cent funded by the US government via the Mutual Weapons Development Agency in Paris. Only much later, in 1960, when the first prototype was halfway through construction, did the UK Government agree to assist with funding of the Hawker prototypes.

In the summer of 1960 this rather odd-looking aircraft – odd at least to the unbelievers – left Kingston on a lorry for Dunsfold aerodrome near Godalming in Surrey, where final assembly and test flying were to take place. But this was test flying with a difference as initially no runway was required, only a steel grid over a large hole in the ground. The P1127, given the serial number XP831, was tethered on the grid which was specially designed to direct the engine efflux away from the engine intakes. Its first 'flight' was to be a hover and, although it was restrained, the cables and strops had sufficient slack in them to allow the aircraft to hover up to a foot or two clear of the grid.

On October 21, 1960, XP831 became airborne for the first time, though for only a few seconds. What a beginning it was: a totally new aircraft type, a new concept, a hover for a first flight, and a pilot with his ankle in plaster: seemingly a recipe for disaster, but it worked. The man who first took the P1127 off the ground, and

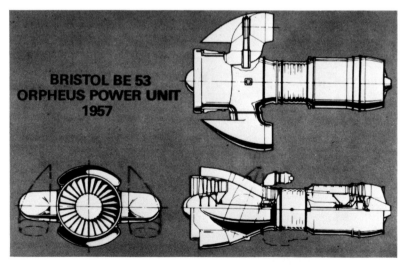

The earliest vectored thrust design, the Bristol BE 53.

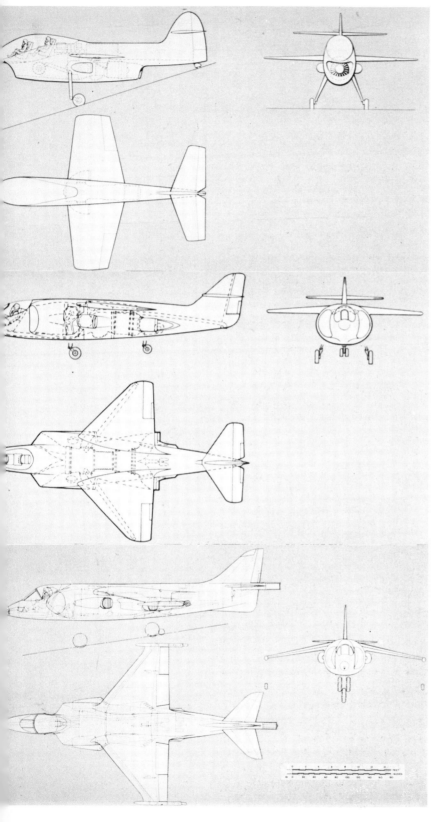

(top) *The configuration of the first P1127 design.*

(middle) *Autumn 1957, the P1127 design becoming practicable.*

(bottom) *General arrangement of the prototype P1127 as issued for manufacture in 1959.*

Within a month of the first tentative hovers, Bill Bedford was accomplishing steady controlled hovering flying within the limits of the tethers which can be seen trailing stark from the nose and outrigger legs. The cable at the rear is for pilot voice communication. The radios were removed to save weight.

later continued to put the aircraft through its flight profiles, was Hawker's chief test pilot, Bill Bedford, now a Regional Marketing Executive based in the Far East for British Aerospace. Involved in a car crash in Germany just prior to the first hover, Bedford was allowed to pilot XP831 as existing rules did not apply to a hover. Because it was in a totally new category of flight, there were no medical regulations for it. In view of this, Bedford was given clearance to fly the aircraft with a broken ankle.

The engine in the aircraft was a Pegasus 2, with a thrust of only 11,000 lb – not much greater than the weight of the aircraft. To ensure the possibility of hover, any item not strictly necessary for the test was removed from XP831 to increase the excess thrust available.

The early hover programme, lasting until late November 1960 and terminating in unrestrained free-air hovers, was followed in March 1961 by the first conventional flight. Then in September of that year, the powered lift and conventional flight modes were dovetailed when the aircraft made its first transition from hover to conventional wingborne flight and vice versa. A total of six P1127s were produced, the last one being the prototype for the next aircraft of the family, the Kestrel.

Mention must be made of another development which became part of the programme at about this time, the P1150 – the first attempt at the design of a supersonic Harrier. This aircraft, which featured the same principles as its subsonic forebears, was designed for an engine with plenum chamber burning (PCB). This was a development of the Bristol engineers and consists of burning fuel in the front pair of nozzles to give a substantial thrust boost for take-off and for supersonic flight.

The P1150 design, in turn, led to the P1154, again a supersonic Harrier-type aircraft powered by a Bristol Siddeley BS100 engine with PCB to 1200 degrees K (1700 degrees F). The P1154 was the winner, in 1962, of the world's biggest international design competition against NATO Basic Military Requirement Number 3

(NBMR-3) for a supersonic V/STOL attack fighter. As the winner of NBMR-3, the P1154 came to be of great interest to both the Royal Air Force and the Royal Navy. However, despite – or perhaps because of – UK Government pressures and Ministry of Defence pleas, each service stuck to its own specific operational requirements for a new V/STOL aircraft.

The RAF wanted a single-seat low-level ground attack/strike fighter with a secondary medium-altitude supersonic intercept capability. The RN specified a two-seat, radar-equipped fighter with all-weather intercept for the primary role and shore/ship attack as a secondary duty, to be catapult-launched from the planned new generation of 50,000 ton carriers. For 18 months, the design team at Kingston struggled to reconcile the conflicting demands of the two services to produce one common aircraft design. This was doomed to failure as there was insufficient common ground between the two service requirements to produce a practical design.

The RN were the first to leave the project, and in 1964 they procured instead the F4 Phantom to provide their future air power at sea. For ten yers from the late 1960s, they successfully operated the F4 from large fleet carriers such as HMS *Ark Royal,* which had steam catapults and arrester gear.

The single-seat RAF version of the P1154, which proceeded into development in late 1963, was finally cancelled in 1965, when the first prototype was about one-third complete. At the time this was disappointing but, taking into account later experiences with subsonic V/STOL, it is doubtful whether the P1154 would have been the best aircraft with which to have introduced V/STOL into service. A supersonic Harrier designed today is very different from the P1154, not least as a result of the practical experience gained by the RAF and RN V/STOL squadrons operating their subsonic Harriers.

The subsonic V/STOL aircraft development, involving the six P1127 prototypes and then the Kestrel, continued alongside the P1154 work from 1962 to 1965. This project came about following an agreement between the governments of the United Kingdom, United States and Federal Republic of Germany for the procurement of nine V/STOL aircraft for service evaluation to assess the practical merits of jet V/STOL in the field. Powered by the improved Pegasus 5 engine of 15,500 lb thrust, the new aircraft was named Kestrel after the British hovering bird of prey, and in 1964 the tripartite squadron came into existence. The Kestrel FGA Mk1 was the first ever jet V/STOL aircraft to be granted a service release, including night flying. The new unit – the Kestrel Evaluation Squadron – with pilots and ground crew drawn from the RAF, US Navy, US Air Force, US Army and the Luftwaffe operated from bases in East Anglia during 1965, evaluating the aircraft on deployments in the field. In total, the squadron notched up 600 flying hours before its work was completed and it was disbanded. The aircraft were assigned to the three member nations, and six of them were shipped in 1966 to the United States where they continued flying under the designation XV-6A. One of these was still flying in the mid-1970s at the NASA Langley Research Centre, Virginia, and is now housed in the splendid new National Air and Space Museum of the Smithsonian Institution in Washington, DC.

The original prototype P1127, XP831, has also survived 12 years of flight testing, including the first jet V/STOL tests on a ship (HMS *Ark Royal,* 1963) and a somewhat spectacular crash (causing little damage) at the Paris Air Show, also in 1963. This aircraft now occupies an honoured position in the Sir Sydney Camm Memorial Hall in the RAF Museum at Hendon, London.

After the cancellation of the P1154 (RAF) in 1965, the UK Government announced that the RAF would be allowed to commence development of an advanced version of Kestrel to enter squadron service in the ground attack and close support roles to replace the ageing Hunter. In 1967 the RAF announced the name of their new aircraft – Harrier (the name that had earlier been reserved for the P1154) and the first version, the GR1, entered service as a ground attack/reconnaissance aircraft with No. 1 (F) Squadron in 1969. The Harrier represented a 90 per cent redesign of the Kestrel and it had the further improved Pegasus 101 engine of 19,000 lb thrust. By 1972, the RAF had formed four frontline Harrier squadrons, three of them based at RAF Wildenrath in the FRG, together with 233 Operational Conversion Unit (OCU) based at RAF Wittering. A year after the GR1 entered service, the first Harrier two-seat trainer – the TMk2 – joined 233 OCU. Although intended to be used principally as a V/STOL trainer, the TMk2 was also designed to have the same weapon capability and combat roles as the single-seat aircraft.

Since the Harrier entered RAF service in 1969 there have been many changes to the aircraft. Notable amongst these has been the increase in engine power from the Pegasus 101 of 19,000 lb through the Pegasus 102 of 20,000 lb to the current Pegasus 103 of 21,500 lb which powers all the RAF Harriers. The RN's Sea Harriers have the more corrosion-resistant Pegasus 104 with the same power output as the 103.

Externally too the RAF Harriers have changed. From the original GR Mk1 and TMk2 aircraft, the re-engining programme brought with it a change in designation, with the Mk1 becoming the Mk3 and the TMk2, the TMk4. In addition the inclusion of laser ranging and marked target-seeker equipment in both types has reshaped the fuselage nose which is more elongated and blunter than the original. Also the aircraft now features a passive radar warning receiver system with the aerials located in the tail.

Interest in the V/STOL spread. The US Marine Corps (USMC) became the first export customer with an eventual order for 102 single-seat Harriers, designated AV-8A in US service, and eight two-seat trainers, designated TAV-8A. The first of these flew in

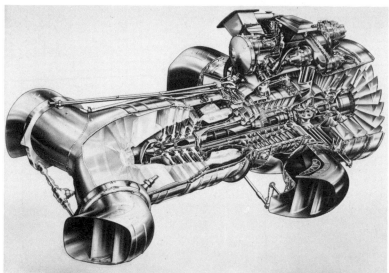

(top) *Four Kestrels of the Tripartite Evaluation Squadron.*

(middle) *The Pegasus engine which powers the Harrier family of V/STOL aircraft.*

(bottom) *XP831, the first vectored thrust fighter demonstrator Harrier now rests in the Sir Sydney Camm Memorial Hall in the RAF Museum at Hendon.*

The Sea Harrier cockpit.

December 1970 and the first USMC AV-8A squadron, VMA 513, was formed in South Carolina in 1971. Since then, the USMC has extensively developed the V/STOL deployment philosophy, operating from austere bases on land, in 'hides', to provide rapid-reaction close support to ground troops, and operating at sea aboard helicopter assault ships such as the USS *Guam* (LPH) class and, latterly the larger USS *Nassau* (LHA) class.

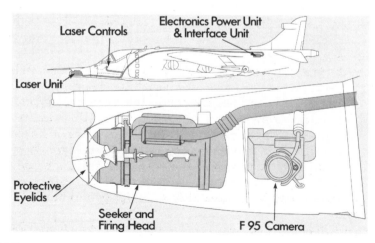

Harrier GR3 nose with the Ferranti Laser Ranging and Marked Target Seeker unit.

Their methods of operation were closely watched and evaluated by the Spanish Navy which operated a wooden-decked World War II vintage carrier, the SNS *Dedalo* (formerly USS *Cabot*). The Spanish Navy saw the need for fixed-wing jet aircraft to complement their maritime forces, which until then had operated only helicopters at sea. Harrier was a natural choice for a service which had never before operated a jet aircraft and which did not aspire to the larger conventional naval aviation carrier with steam catapults and arrester gear. The Harrier was, and remains, the only jet aircraft in the western world that can safely launch and recover from a flat deck with no associated mechanical assistance. Final proof of the aircraft's capabilities came for the Spanish Navy when a Harrier took off from Dunsfold in 1972 and flew direct to SNS *Dedalo*, which was under way off the Spanish coast near Barcelona. SNS *Dedalo* has a wooden deck and there were many who thought that the Harrier's jets would scorch the planking, if not set fire to the timber. As it turned out, this fear proved unfounded. The jets did not even discolour the planking though they did melt and smear the waterproofing pitch in the joints. For the future, however, a metal plate was added to the carrier's deck for vertical take-off and landing, and later the entire stern section of the deck was overlaid with metal sheeting. Once the decision had been taken to adopt V/STOL in 1975, the Spanish Navy sent ten of its best helicopter pilots to the United States for training, first as conventional jet pilots and then on to V/STOL conversion. In total each flew some 200 hours while in the United States.

In parallel with the training programme, six Harriers, similar to the USMC's AV-8A, and two two-seaters, similar to the TAV-8A, were purchased by the US Government and delivered to the United States in 1976. They were resold to the Spanish Government and used by the Spanish pilots during the latter stages of their training programme in the United States – when SNS *Dedalo* arrived in US waters for flying training operations. The *Dedalo* returned to Spain with the aircraft aboard. In Spanish Navy service, the Harrier is named Matador, and the aircraft are based at Rota in southern Spain, with regular deployments aboard SNS *Dedalo* during exercises with other units of the Spanish fleet and the Spanish Air Force.

Since the first batch of eight aircraft, the Matador Squadron has taken delivery of a further five single-seat AV-8S aircraft. A second group of pilots were later trained in the United Kingdom. In May 1982, Spain's new carrier, the sea-control ship *Principe de Asturias*, was launched at her building yard in Ferrol, north Spain. She features a 12 degree ski-jump integrated most elegantly with the basic hull design, in a way that rather shames the add-on crudity exhibited by the ramps on HMS *Invincible, Illustrious* and *Hermes,* all of which were fitted after the ships had basically been completed.

As a result of a UK Government go-ahead in 1975, the RN's Sea

117

Harrier emerged in 1978. Externally, the Sea Harrier differs little from the other aircraft of the Harrier family except for the re-designed nose and raised cockpit. It has, however, a completely new avionics fit for its maritime roles and missions, including the Ferranti Blue Fox radar as the primary air-to-air and air-to-surface mission sensor.

The RN decision to opt for a navalised version of the Harrier has its origins back in the 1960s, when the RN were operating their F4 Phantoms from the decks of such ships as HMS *Eagle,* HMS *Victorious* and HMS *Ark Royal.* In 1966, following the UK Government's announcement that a new carrier known as CVA-01 was never to be built, it appeared that the Fleet Air Arm's future role would be reduced to that of helicopter operator and that RN surface ships would have to rely on the RAF to provide tactical air cover from land bases. Fortunately this politically based view – that tactical air cover provided by aircraft flying from land bases could be an effective alternative to naval combat aircraft flying from surface ships – was proved untenable, most recently by the Falklands campaign, and turned out to be short-lived.

The RN had shown interest in V/STOL from the early days, when the first prototype P1127, XP831, operated briefly aboard *Ark Royal* in 1963. Since that time, aircraft of the Harrier family have flown from the decks of over 40 ships of 9 nations, ranging from large attack carriers, through cruisers and assault ships, down to supply vessels such as Royal Fleet Auxiliaries. The interest shown by the RN in the V/STOL Harrier changed to positive need when the announcement came that the *Ark Royal* type of carrier would not be replaced and that the F4 and Buccaneer squadrons were to be disbanded when existing carriers eventually came to the end of their hull life. In the early 1970s it was foreseen that the demise of HMS *Ark Royal* (the last of her breed) would occur in the second half of the decade.

The Sea Harrier was to operate from the latest carriers of the *Invincible* class, as well as from the only surviving conventional flat top, HMS *Hermes.* During her design and building periods, at the time when the term 'carrier' had been politically discredited, HMS *Invincible* had been variously referred to as a 'through deck cruiser', 'command cruiser' and 'anti-submarine cruiser'. Nevertheless, she was and is still a carrier, regardless of her other roles. She was orginally conceived in the late 1960s for use by a ro-tary wing air group and was already under construction when the RN received approval for the procurement of the first 24 Sea Harriers. The influence of jet V/STOL on the ship's design has therefore been minimal.

In *Invincible* and in *Illustrious,* the second ship of the class, the ski-jump ramp is limited to 7 degrees due to the positioning of the Sea Dart missile launcher at the front of the flight deck. It proved impossible to move the launcher at an advanced stage of the ships' construction when the ski-jump was being adopted by the RN as a

The new Harrier II on test in the USA. It is due to enter service with the USMC as the AV-8B and later with the RAF as the GRMk5.

launching aid. The third ship of the class, the new HMS *Ark Royal* (at one time to be named HMS *Indomitable*), was not even laid down until the late 1970s and she therefore has a 12 degree ski-jump, as does *Hermes* following her refit in 1980-81.

All the RN carriers carry peacetime air groups of five Sea Harriers and ten Sea King ASW helicopters. However, in the South Atlantic HMS *Invincible* operated a fixed-wing air group of twice her planned number, while *Hermes* operated over four times the number of Harriers she would normally have carried.

Since the Sea Harrier FRS Mk1 entered service in 1979, a number of RN squadrons have been formed. The first unit, which saw the introduction of the aircraft, was 700A (the Intensive Flying Trials Unit), distinguishable by a large 'A' on the Sea Harrier's fin. This unit was disbanded in 1981 and immediately re-formed as 899 Naval Air Squadron, the Headquarters Unit responsible for training. The first Sea Harrier operational unit to form (in 1980) was 800 Squadron. It has operated at sea, mostly using *Hermes* as its parent ship. In 1981, 801 Naval Air Squadron became the second frontline unit and normally operates from HMS *Invincible*. Finally, 809 Naval Air Squadron was formed for the duration of the Falklands conflict and is now disbanded.

Who would have guessed that the small, rather squat design of 1957 could have matured into the Sea Harrier of today? By no stretch of the imagination does the Sea Harrier flaunt the eye-catching slinky looks of conventional needle-nosed supersonic fighters; but it does have a magic all of its own. It has always been a show-stopper to the general public, and is both highly regarded by those who fly it and enormously respected by adversary pilots. Yet it remained the subject of many misconceptions. Now, however, it has been proven in combat, 25 years after its original conception.

There were losses in the South Atlantic. That was inevitable. But most of these were caused either by the appalling weather conditions or as a result of heavy ground fire due to the need for low flying in support of ground forces. The Harriers were never bested in air-to-air combat, even by the supersonic aggressors pitched against them.

The role of the RAF Harrier in land-based operations

The RAF Harrier GR3s are deployed primarily in the ground attack and reconnaissance roles in support of NATO ground forces. They are not fighters, unlike the Sea Harrier which has to take on a wider spectrum of duties, including that of air defence. The Spanish Navy's Matador role from ships is similar, but the AV-8As of the US Marine Corps (USMC) tend to take duties parallel to those of the RAF's GR3s, primarily being used in the ground attack role.

To the RAF, the Harrier offers a unique capability and one that is utilised a great deal – its lack of reliance on a conventional runway. Conventional attack aircraft which depend on concrete runways for launch and recovery could, in the circumstances of war, become very limited in their operational capabilities. A runway cannot be hidden. It has a known location and is already pre-targeted by a potential enemy. It cannot be moved and only one or two runway denial missiles will put it and its complement of conventional aircraft out of effective action. Nor can a runway be adequately defended, either by guns or surface-to-air-missile systems – the base area involved is too big. And what defence is

Only the Harrier could have landed on an airfield so damaged and still remain fully operational.

possible against short-range surface-to-surface-missiles? A runway for conventional military jets is at least 8,000 ft long. That is a large target and just one or two craters will render it inoperable to almost all current fast jet tactical aircraft. Craters can be filled in a short time, but this is no easy proposition if the hole is small and gives off a distinct tick, for delayed action ordnance is a normal operational tactic. Further, if the aircraft have already left and the airfield attack was too late to prevent them from launching, how and where would they recover? Instant concrete has to be really quick-setting if the holes appear while the squadrons are airborne. If there is no friendly base within range either the pilot attempts to crash or force-land his aircraft on or near the runway, or he ejects. Each is a less than satisfactory solution in the tactical air-power battle.

A runway has no dependable place in today's tactical warfare. In only a matter of hours it will be put out of action by any number of runway denial weapons. The ideal is to be able to spread aircraft around a number of sites, preferably well away from runways, and rely on their capability in short or vertical take-off. Harrier is currently the *only* aircraft that can meet this need.

Regularly, and for periods of many days at a time, the RAF Harriers in Germany leave their main base at Gutersloh and with minimal ground support deploy from sites deep in the heart of the German countryside. Not only does this field deployment enable the Harriers to operate much closer to the 'frontline', but the sites are very hard to locate and would demand extreme effort from an adversary. Should a site be discovered, or be thought to have been located, it is a straightforward task to move the aircraft and their ground support to another site.

These sites can be a 'hide' housing only one Harrier with no ground support at all – the Harrier has a self-starting capability and therefore needs no external support equipment if only waiting to carry out one mission – or a more complex affair, with refuelling, re-arming and servicing capabilities, housing four to six Harriers.

A pilot dispersing from his main base in times of emergency would fly to his one-aircraft 'hide', land, taxi in under cover from aerial reconnaissance, shut down his engine and await the order to launch. Once the order to launch has been received, the pilot will start up and taxi his aircraft out to the area where he can carry out short or vertical take-off, depending on the site. From launch, he will fly to his target, carry out the attack and recover to either a corner of his main base or to the intermediate site, which could be a complex of 'hides' with refuelling and re-arming capabilities supporting a group of Harriers.

This same principle is also used by the USMC, for though each service differs in operational details and requirements, both need to fly combat missions from rudimentary bases or sites and both have a vital need to reduce the reaction time between the call for air support and the actual arrival of that aircraft over the targeted

Harrier GR3's of No 1 Squadron.

RAF Harriers operating in Norway suitably camouflaged for the winter conditions.

position. Experience in the USMC during the Vietnam War proved that air support with conventional aircraft flying from a main base many miles to the rear, or from a carrier some miles off the coastline, could mean a reaction delay of 40–60 minutes. In modern warfare, speed of movement and rapidly changing local tactical fortunes could mean that the aircraft delivers too much ordnance, too late. Even worse, as has sadly occurred, the ordnance could fall on a friendly unit that had moved into the area during reaction delay time. Quite often, between the call for conventional air support and its arrival, even the weather will change over the target and therefore negate the planning and military effort. The USMC therefore attach great importance to rapid reaction and the fire support service provided by their forward-based V/STOL Harriers.

While the RAF Harriers are deployed from concealed sites, whether single 'hides' or intermediate field bases, their sorties rate is very high. For example on a field exercise in Germany which involved 28 Harriers, a total of 1,120 missions were flown in only nine days. In another exercise, in the United Kingdom, 12 Harriers flew an average of over 10 sorties per day over a 3-day period. Not only do these results demonstrate the military productivity of the Harrier but also they say much for the serviceability and durability of the aircraft, as the Harriers were exposed to weather in the most primitive of field conditions, akin to the days of the Royal Flying Corps in World War I and totally alien to the experiences of today's modern tactical air forces.

To return to the importance of fast reaction, when the front line infantry call for air support, they need it quickly and only a forward based jet V/STOL aircraft can provide the speed of response and the quantity of weaponry needed in such a short time. Its flight time is measured as only a few minutes. When it does arrive, it will be flying at 250 ft or lower, at speeds of 400–500 knots. The pilot will deliver his weapons and be gone before the bulk of the ground-to-air defences can train their guns or missiles. This mode of attack ensures the highest possible survival rate, as was proved in the Falklands.

All of the three RAF Harrier GR3s lost over the Falklands fell to ground gunfire. One of these was still flying 100 miles or so later when it was forced to ditch, en route back to the ship, through lack of fuel. Another kept going for some time, enabling the pilot to clear strongly held enemy territory. Both pilots ejected successfully and were recovered unharmed. In the third incident, the pilot ejected over Argentine-held territory, was captured and became the only British prisoner-of-war.

The RAF has no formal requirement that the GR3 be a fighter, although, armed with Sidewinder and 30 mm Aden guns, it is more than capable of defending itself. The USMC on the other hand require the aircraft to be a fighter as well as a ground attack aircraft and, in the early 1970s, they instigated a programme to look into

A single seat and a two seat Harrier — designated Matador – in Spanish Navy service.

the advantages of using engine nozzle rotation in combat. The result, after a couple of years work, was thrust Vectoring In Forward Flight (VIFF) which entails using the nozzles to improve the aircraft's manoeuvrability – either to slow down and force an opponent to overshoot, or to turn inside him, or to pitch up the nose very rapidly for a 'snapshot' action. VIFF is exclusive to the Harrier family of aircraft. Following the work done by the USMC in the early 1970s, VIFF has been enthusiastically adopted by all the Harrier users, the RAF and the RN as well as by the Spanish Matador pilots. The enormous surprise factor it provides, combined with the inherently high manoeuvrability and excess power of the Harrier family of aircraft, particularly at the lower altitudes, have enabled astonishing success to be scored in peacetime combat exercises against powerful contemporary supersonic fighters such as the F-4, F-14, F-15, F-16 and F-5, as well as NATO Mirage squadrons. However, the combat conditions over the

A Harrier II with RAF markings. When it enters UK service the aircraft will be designated GR5.

Falklands allowed no real advantage to be gained by VIFF. Combats were mostly at low level at speeds of around 550 knots and involved high g turns and hard breaks in an essentially horizontal plane.

The USMC's experience with the AV-8A, Harrier, delivered in the early 1970s led in 1976 to the requirement for an improved Harrier, which is to enter service in the mid-1980s. The full designation in USMC service is the AV-8B Harrier II, and some 340 are planned. They will equip all the USMC's attack squadrons and from 1986 gradually take over the role at present filled by the A4 Skyhawks. The RAF is also to order the Harrier II with a requirement for 60. These will be designated Harrier GR5 and they will be deployed from the late 1980s alongside the GR Mk3s in the NATO theatre, in support of ground forces.

The Harrier II is the result of a joint collaborative programme between British Aerospace and McDonnell Douglas in which the latter is the prime contractor for the USMC order and BAe is the main subcontractor. For the RAF order, the roles are reversed. In both cases the prime contractor is responsible for final assembly, test flight and delivery.

An operational view of the Sea Harrier

The Sea Harrier can fly its maximum weight missions from a flat-deck runway of 600 ft in winds over deck (WOD) greater than 25 knots. But, if the ship is fitted with a ski-jump at the bows, this deck roll can be reduced by more than 50 per cent yet still permit retention of the same payload. Alternatively, with a full 600 ft take-off run via a ski-jump, up to 30 per cent more fuel or ordnance may be carried.

Ski-jump can be exploited fully only by a vectored thrust aircraft. Its advantages are many. A navy which cannot afford a fleet carrier with steam catapults, etc., can, with a much smaller ship fitted with a ski-jump, launch V/STOL aircraft for effective air operations. A conventional carrier, retrofitted with a ski-jump, can operate V/STOL attack aircraft at much less operating and maintenance costs than would be incurred when flying conventional naval combat aircraft. Such a converted carrier could continue in effective service for many years. HMS *Hermes* is an ideal example of this, being still in service when her former sister ships are scrapped and gone.

Ski-jump launches are safer than conventional flat-deck launches since the aircraft leaves the carrier deck in an upward trajectory. The time provided by this upward launch enables the V/STOL aircraft to accelerate sufficiently to a speed where wing lift and thrust combine to equal the weight. The upward momentum provided by the ramp also allows the pilot a much greater margin of time should something go wrong and he is forced to eject. The rotatable nozzles enable the aircraft to transition smoothly from powered lift to wingborne flight after leaving the ski-jump, just as they do from a flat deck or runway launch, so that no new techniques are needed by the pilot. Indeed, pilot workload when launching from the ramp is considerably less than in a flat-deck STO and therefore the ski-jump provides additional safety and dependability as well as the considerable performance boost of substantially more military load from a fixed deck run or much reduced deck run or WOD for a given military load.

Sea Harriers using ski-jump can launch in rapid succession – typically a complete squadron of five aircraft within two minutes. Apart from safety and speed of launch, ski-jump also brings another advantage. It can be used operationally by a pilot who has never before flown from the deck of a carrier – again witness the RAF GR3s in *Hermes*. Many of the RAF Falklands pilots had never been on a carrier, let alone launched from a deck in war.

Just as important, V/STOL at sea provides naval operations with an air group flexibility hitherto unknown in maritime history. There is no reason why the Harrier's ability to operate independently and in confined areas on land should not be translated to a naval environment. Using the same principle as the RAF in its operations in central Europe, naval command now has the option of using the carrier in the same way that the RAF regards its main base. From such a main base in a fleet or task force, the Sea Harrier can deploy to other decks either on fighting ships or on merchant ships or fleet support vessels. Almost any deck capable of carrying a Sea King helicopter, for example, can, if necessary, become a Sea Harrier deck.

For example, a Sea Harrier launched from the carrier to the outer edge of the fleet or task force could land and refuel on a totally different type of ship such as a Royal Fleet Auxiliary, an assault ship or destroyer/large frigate/cruiser-type ship. It could also be diverted to one of these types in an emergency, if the carrier had been damaged or perhaps if the flight deck was so full there was no room to recover another aircraft temporarily. With Sea Harrier, the luxury of being able to recover to another deck when out of range of shore bases is a reality. No other naval fixed-wing aircraft enjoys this flexibility.

The runway width in the Royal Navy's V/STOL carriers is some 45 ft (14 m). No hazard is presented by the Harriers in full- throttle STO launches to men or equipment on the flight deck outside the wingtip safety lines, which are some 22.5 ft (7 m) from the centreline of the take-off path. Harriers are marshalled for multiple launch with successive aircraft separated on the runway at about 100 ft (30 m) intervals. The lead Harrier, launching down the deck at full power, constitutes no hazard to the aircraft standing behind it on the runway. This technique allows rapid sequential launches to be achieved at intervals as low as 15 seconds.

In the course of the Falklands campaign, a number of developments were tried out which will become an integral part of the Harrier story in the future. One of the most important of these was the use of merchant ships to augment the theatre tactical airpower capacity. *Atlantic Conveyor* became the best-known of these ships. A container/ro-ro ship, she was used as a Harrier transport vessel and was converted to this role in only three days, carrying eight Sea Harriers and six GR3s to the fleet in the South Atlantic in addition to helicopters and many other vital stores and equipment. Another such vessel which acted as a Harrier 'garage ship' was the *Contender Bezant*.

Since the mid-1970s studies in the United Kingdom and the United States have looked at the use of commercial container ships as auxiliary helicopter and aircraft carriers in emergencies. The modern container ship offers an ideal basic configuration – a long unobstructed top deck and high speed. With very little obstruction to the peacetime use of such a ship a suitable runway could be provided for the aircraft by the emplacement of rapidly rigged decking, supported by the top layer of containers. It has been shown that such a ship could, in time of war, augment a fleet's carrier force at a fraction of the cost of a standard 'flat top'.

This analysis was at least partly proved when the *Atlantic Conveyor* was chosen as a Harrier transport ship. She differed from the full concept in that she did not feature a full-length runway, nor did she have a ski-jump because there was simply insufficient time in April 1982 for a full conversion. But she did prove that the approach was sound and practical. Even though she was later sunk, her destruction was in part due to her having no defences as well as to her being unable to take any evasive action.

Satisfaction with the Sea Harrier's basic capability operating from ships has led the UK to an intended programme of updating the aircraft to ensure that it remains operationally competitive to the end of the century.

These proposed improvements are known as the Sea Harrier Mid-Life Update programme and foremost among the changes envisaged is the inclusion of a new Ferranti Pulse Doppler Radar which, together with present day and future air-to-air missiles, will give the aircraft a 'look-down/shoot-down' capability. The radar antenna will be bigger than that of the current Blue Fox radar, and will be housed in an enlarged nose.

Artist impression of Mid-Life Update improvements proposed for the Sea Harrier.

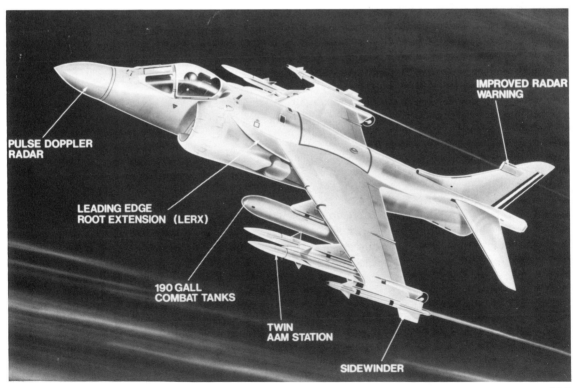

A Sea Harrier during qualifying trials launching from a land-based ski-jump at RAE Bedford, with two Sea Eagle anti-ship missiles.

Already equipped with 190 gallon drop tanks as a result of BAe's intensive industrial efforts during the Falklands crisis, the Sea Harrier's capability as a naval fighter could be further enhanced by the inclusion of twin stations for AMRAAM (Advanced Medium Range Air-to-Air Missile) on the outer wing pylons. Redesign of the wing tip would also allow two additional weapon stations on the aircraft, for the carriage of Sidewinder or ASRAAM (Advanced Short Range Air-to-Air Missile).

In addition to carriage of a full range of standard UK, US and NATO ordnance, Sea Harrier's anti-ship strike capability will be greatly enhanced when the newly developed BAe Sea Eagle, a stand-off, sea-skimming, air-to-surface anti-ship missile, enters service with the Royal Navy. Sea Eagle is a long range anti-ship missile more than a generation ahead of Exocet in terms of electronic sophistication and performance and is due to see service on Sea Harriers as well as RAF Buccaneers.

Sea Harrier does not require deck catapult launch or arrested landing. It can operate effectively from much smaller ships than are required by conventional naval combat aircraft.

Spurred by the use of merchant ships as Harrier carriers during the Falklands campaign, BAe has recently completed the initial study of a Shipborne Containerised Air Defence System (SCADS). The concept is predicated on the containerisation of several military systems – Sea Harrier support facilities, Sea Wolf anti-missile system(s), air defence/surveillance radar, active missile countermeasures and, if required, ASW helicopter support. Medium Girder Bridge elements are used for the Harrier runway and Ski-Jump. A total of about 230 containers are needed for a full installation which would include command and control facilities, accommodation units for some 190 men and self-contained power and water supplies as well as logistic support for about 30 days' operations at sea.

The containerised systems would be suitable for carriage on a variety of commercial containerships upwards of 30,000 dead-weight tonnes. The study shows that the ship could be rigged and ready to proceed to sea after about two days' work. For an investment which amounts to a small fraction of that required for an equivalent warship, it is possible to provide integral combat air-power at sea with a task force or convoy in circumstances where existing fighting ships are liable to be committed elsewhere.

The Falklands campaign was the proving ground for V/STOL. Both the RN's Sea Harriers and the RAF's GR3s operated in appalling weather, in which conventional fighter aircraft would have been grounded. The aircraft withstood battle damage and proved simple to repair. But the most striking outcome of the entire campaign as far as the Sea Harrier is concerned was the incredibly high serviceability provided by this small group of overworked aircraft operating from just two carriers. Even during the early periods of the campaign, figures of 80–85 per cent availability were being reported. At the end of the conflict, initial Government sources confirmed 85 per cent overall. Later that figure

Shipbourne Containerised Air Defense System (SCADS). A study of the use of merchant ships as Harrier carriers and other military systems.

rose to an astonishing 95 per cent, and has since been confirmed by air engineering officers of the Sea Harrier squadrons in the two carriers.

The experiences of the Falklands are still being evaluated, but one of the early decisions taken by the UK Government after the ceasefire was to order an additional 14 Sea Harriers for the RN and also to announce the intention of replacing all the RAF GR3s that were lost. In addition, it was proved conclusively that it is impractical to operate only two carriers within the fleet. This has resulted in a stay of execution for *Invincible,* which was at one time to be sold or leased to Australia, and for *Hermes* which had an undecided future. Whether *Hermes* will be sold overseas remains to be seen. The new Government of Australia has decided that the RAN will not continue with fixed-wing air power from carriers. It is now agreed in the UK that three carriers will continue in service thus guaranteeing that at least two ships will be in commission and available at any time.

And what of the Sea Harrier squadron strength of five aircraft? Is this sufficient to provide optimum efficiency and capability? Some pilots say not and are pressing for an increase in the number of aircraft per squadron – seven or even eight would be the optimum, they argue. Whether this will be, remains to be seen. But at quarter-century of practical jet V/STOL saw many doubters and much disbelief in the Harrier and its capabilities. The concept has too many penalties, they claimed, compared with conventional military jets. Harrier was a splendid aircraft for air shows they said: the crowd loves it and everybody applauds. But it will never be any good in a fight. How wrong they were.